Practice Questions and Answers for The Life in the UK Test

Published by Garuda Publications and available from:

Garuda Publications
41 Beech Close
Walton-on-Thames
Surrey KT12 5RQ, UK
Email: Sales@GarudaPublications.com
www.GarudaPublications.com

Cover design Goran J. Tomic

ISBN 978-1-9996650-1-2

Edited by: Andrew Thompson

Printed by Page Bros Group, Norwich, UK

You can study for the Life in the UK Test with our sister publication:
The Life in the UK Test Handbook: Essential independent guide on the test for 'Settlement in the UK' and 'British Citizenship', 4th edition

Free Online Interactive E-learning Book and Practice Tests

Create an account at *Training.Garudapublications.com*. Then use the enrollment key **Garuda2017** to gain free access to the E-learning training and practice tests - currently for up to 5 days. *Garuda Publications reserves the right to vary the free term and enrollment keys without prior notice.*

CONTENTS

INTRODUCTION

This book presents 25 full practice tests (600 questions) for The Life in the UK Test. Each practice test consists of 24 multiple choice questions – the same as in the real test. The four question types used in these practice tests are the same as in the actual test.

All the questions in this guide are based on the contents of the official study material for the test 'Life in the United Kingdom: A Guide for New Residents'. The questions will help you check your understanding of the study material in preparation for the official test.

The pass mark for the Life in the UK Test is 75% so you need to get 18 out of the 24 questions correct, within the 45 minutes allowed, in order to pass.

Each practice test is followed by a page showing the correct answers.

HOW TO PREPARE FOR THE TEST

The Home Office does not publish the official questions for the Life in the UK Test so any independently produced question set will not be exactly the same as in the real test. For this reason reason we always advise students to read and revise the official study material rather than trying to memorize practice questions and answers.

Practice tests can prove very useful to familiarise students with the question types and to help them to check their understanding of the study material. Generally, treat preparing for the Life in the UK Test as you would any exam.

THE FOUR QUESTION TYPES

There are four types of multiple choice question in the test.

The 'official' example questions are reproduced below:

Question type 1 - *Select one correct answer from four options*

Example

Who is the patron saint of Scotland?

    A. St Andrew

    B. St George

    C. St David

    D. St Patrick

(Answer = A = St Andrew)

Question type 2 - *Decide whether a statement is true or false*

Example

Is the statement below TRUE or FALSE?

You have to be at least 21 years old before you can serve on a jury.

(Answer = False)

Question type 3 - *Select two correct answers from four options*

[You have to pick two answers]

What is the name of the TWO houses that make up the UK Parliament?

    A. House of the People

    B. House of Commons

    C. House of Lords

    D. House of Government

(Answer = B & C = House of Commons; and House of Lords)

Question type 4 - *Select the correct statement from a choice of two statements*

Example

Which of these statements is correct?

    A. Nelson was a famous British military leader who died at the Battle of Trafalgar.

    B. Nelson was a famous British military leader who died at the Battle of Waterloo.

(Answer = A = Nelson died at Trafalgar)

PRACTICE TEST 1

Question 1
How many years ago did a land bridge permanently separate Britain from the continent by the Channel?

    A. About 1 million years ago

    B. About 10,000 years ago

    C. During the Bronze Age

    D. During the Iron Age

Question 2
Is the statement below True or False?

The UK is made up of England, Scotland, Wales and Northern Ireland.

Question 3
Which is not one of the main political parties?

    A. The Conservative Party

    B. The Labour Party

    C. The Liberal Democrats

    D. The Democratic Unionist Party

Question 4
Is the statement below True or False?

More men than women study at university.

Question 5
Which of these statements is correct?

    A. The UK is made up of England, Scotland and Wales.

    B. The UK is made up of England, Scotland, Wales and Northern Ireland.

Question 6

What is the Life in the UK test study material designed to help you to do?

    A. To help you to integrate into society and play a full role in your local community

    B. To reduce the number of people able to come to the UK

    C. To make sure you can demonstrate a minimum academic level

    D. To help you with the citizenship process

Question 7

What are the TWO types of peers found in the House of Lords?

    A. Hereditary peers

    B. Crown peers

    C. Life peers

    D. Common peers

Question 8

Which of these statements is correct?

    A. The people of the Iron Age made the first coins to be minted in Britain.

    B. The people of the Bronze Age made the first coins to be minted in Britain.

Question 9

Which of these statements is correct?

    A. You have to be over 21 to go into betting shops or gambling clubs

    B. You have to be over 18 to go into betting shops or gambling clubs

Question 10

Identify TWO of the fundamental principles of British life below:

    A. The rule of law

    B. Individual liberty

    C. Volunteering

    D. Protest

Question 11

Which of these statements is correct?

- A. At the Opening of Parliament the Queen makes a speech which summarises the government's policies for the year ahead.
- B. At Trooping the Colour the Queen makes a speech which summarizes the government's policies for the year ahead.

Question 12

Which of these statements is correct?

- A. The Speaker is neutral and does not represent a political party.
- B. The Prime Minister is neutral and does not represent a political party.

Question 13

Is the statement below True or False?

Post-war immigration means that nearly 10% of the population has a parent or grandparent born outside the UK.

Question 14

Which TWO roman generals invaded Britain in 55BC and then AD43?

- A. Julius Caesar
- B. Nero
- C. Claudius
- D. Tiberius

Question 15

Is the statement below True or False?

The Canterbury Tales, written in English by Geoffrey Chaucer, was one of the first books to be printed.

Question 16

Which group petitioned Parliament for the right to vote for the working classes and those without property?

A. The Levellers

B. The Luddites

C. The Covenanters

D. The Chartists

Question 17

Is the statement below True or False?

Ann Boleyn, wife of Henry VIII and mother to Elizabeth I, was beheaded.

Question 18

What does the Muslim Eid al-Fitr celebrate?

A. The birth of Jesus Christ

B. The end of Ramadan

C. The founding of the community known as Khalsa

D. The victory of good over evil and the gaining of knowledge

Question 19

Who chairs debates in the House of Commons?

A. The Moderator

B. The Speaker

C. The Chair

D. The Leader of the House

Question 20

Which flowers are worn on Remembrance Day?

A. Lilies'

B. Poppies

C. Daffodils

D. Roses

Question 21

Which of these statements is correct?

    A. In 1833 the Emancipation Act abolished slavery throughout the British Empire.

    B. In 1833 the Freedom Act abolished slavery throughout the British Empire.

Question 22

Which TWO of Henry VIII's daughters went onto be Queens of England?

    A. Elizabeth

    B. Mary

    C. Jane

    D. Matilda

Question 23

Which TWO of these are Christian festivals?

    A. Christmas Day

    B. Hanukkah

    C. Easter

    D. Bonfire Night

Question 24

Is the statement below True or False?

The UK has a free press.

Practice Test 1 – Answers

Question 1 - B

Question 2 - True

Question 3 - D

Question 4 - FALSE

Question 5 - B

Question 6 - A

Question 7 - A & C

Question 8 - A

Question 9 - B

Question 10 - A & B

Question 11 - A

Question 12 - A

Question 13 - True

Question 14 - A & C

Question 15 - True

Question 16 - D

Question 17 - True

Question 18 - B

Question 19 - B

Question 20 - B

Question 21 - A

Question 22 - A & B

Question 23 - A & C

Question 24 - True

PRACTICE TEST 2

Question 1

In Northern Ireland the anniversary of which battle is celebrated as a public holiday?

    A. The Battle of Trafalgar

    B. The Battle of The Somme

    C. The Battle of Killecrankie

    D. The Battle of The Boyne

Question 2

Is the statement below True or False?

'Great Britain' refers only to England, Scotland and Wales.

Question 3

Which of these statements is correct?

    A. Alan Turing is a famous scientist who showed how gravity applied to the whole universe.

    B. Isaac Newton is a famous scientist who showed how gravity applied to the whole universe.

Question 4

How many Indians fought on behalf of Britain in the First World War?

    A. None

    B. A few thousand

    C. More than a million

    D. Around eight million

Question 5

Is the statement below True or False?

Boxing Day is the day before Christmas Day.

Question 6

Which of these statements is correct?

   A. Sir Robert Walpole was the first Prime Minister.

   B. Lloyd George was the first Prime Minister.

Question 7

Who set up the Women's Franchise League in 1889 which fought to get the vote in local elections for married women?

   A. Florence Nightingale

   B. Queen Victoria

   C. Emmeline Pankhurst

   D. Ellie Simmonds

Question 8

Where were the Paralympics games hosted in 2012?

   A. London

   B. Liverpool

   C. Manchester

   D. Glasgow

Question 9

Is the statement below True or False?

Civil servants are politically neutral.

Question 10

Which TWO from the list below are notable British sportsmen and women?

   A. Roger Bannister

   B. William Walton

   C. Kelly Holmes

   D. Harold Wilson

Question 11

What are the proceedings of Parliament published in?

    A. Parliamentary Proceedings

    B. Parliament Magazine

    C. The Domesday Book

    D. Hansard

Question 12

Which of these statements is correct?

    A. The House of Commons is regarded as the more important of the two chambers in Parliament because its members are democratically elected.

    B. The House of Lords is regarded as the more important of the two chambers in Parliament because its members are democratically elected.

Question 13

Is the statement below True or False?

King Charles I army was defeated at the Battles of Marston Moor and Naseby.

Question 14

Which TWO things is Queen Elizabeth II head of state of?

    A. The head of state of the UK

    B. The head of state for many countries in the Commonwealth

    C. The head of state of the European Union

    D. The head of state of NATO

Question 15

Identify TWO of the things that the UK offers in return for individuals fulfilling their citizenship responsibilities.

    A. Freedom of speech

    B. A right to a fair trial

    C. Employment

    D. Healthcare

Question 16

Which of these statements is correct?

A. The Foreign Secretary is responsible for managing relationships with foreign countries.

B. The International Relations Secretary is responsible for managing relationships with foreign countries.

Question 17

Which TWO tribes from Northern Europe invade Britain when the Roman army left in AD410?

A. Vikings

B. Jutes

C. Angles

D. Normans

Question 18

Is the statement below True or False?

England has never won the World Cup

Question 19

Which of these statements is correct?

A. The chairperson of the Church of Scotland is the Moderator and is appointed for one year only.

B. The chairperson of the Church of Scotland is the Justice of the Peace and is appointed for one year only.

Question 20

Is the statement below True or False?

As France fell, during the Second World War, Britain evacuated 300,000 men from the beaches around Calais.

Question 21

Which of these statements is correct?

    A. 'Great Britain' refers only to England, Scotland and Wales.

    B. 'Great Britain' refers only to England and Scotland.

Question 22

Where is the Welsh Government based?

    A. Sheffield

    B. Cardiff

    C. Edinburgh

    D. London

Question 23

Which of these statements is correct?

    A. In the 2009 citizenship survey about one fifth (21%) of people said they had no religion.

    B. In the 2009 citizenship survey about half (50%) of people said they had no religion.

Question 24

What were the TWO key battles that king Charles I army was defeated at in the Civil war?

    A. Cropredy Bridge

    B. Edge hill

    C. Marston Moor

    D. Naseby

Practice Test 2 – Answers

Question 1 - D

Question 2 -True

Question 3 - B

Question 4 - C

Question 5 - False

Question 6 - A

Question 7 - C

Question 8 - A

Question 9 - True

Question 10 - A & C

Question 11 - D

Question 12 - A

Question 13 - True

Question 14 - A & B

Question 15 - A & B

Question 16 - A

Question 17 - B & C

Question 18 - False

Question 19 - A

Question 20 - False

Question 21 - A

Question 22 - B

Question 23 - A.

Question 24 - C & D

PRACTICE TEST 3

Question 1
Is the statement below True or False?

Margaret Thatcher was a prominent suffragette

Question 2
Which of these statements is correct?

    A. Father's day is the third Saturday in July.

    B. Father's day is the third Sunday in June.

Question 3
Which TWO are British inventions of the 20th century?

    A. The Jet Engine

    B. The Light bulb

    C. Radar

    D. The Rocket

Question 4
What momentous change happened in Ireland in 1921?

    A. Ireland declared unilateral independence

    B. Ireland became two countries (Irish Free State and Northern Ireland)

    C. Ireland joined the European Union

    D. Ireland joined the Euro

Question 5
Since when has the UK had a fully democratic voting system?

    A. 1918

    B. 1928

    C. 1969

    D. 2000

Question 6

Is the statement below True or False?

Composer Benjamin Britten is best known for his operas which include Peter Grimes and Billy Bud.

Question 7

Which of these statements is correct?

A. In 1314 the Scottish, led by Robert the Bruce, defeated the English at the Battle of Bannockburn keeping Scotland unconquered.

B. In 1314 the Scottish, led by Robert the Bruce, defeated the English at the Battle of the Boyne keeping Scotland unconquered.

Question 8

How did car ownership change between 1930 and 1939?

A. It stagnated – staying at round 1 million

B. It showed continuous steady growth

C. It slumped – from 2 million to 1 million

D. It doubled – from 1 million to 2 million

Question 9

Is the statement below True or False?

In Scotland a jury decides on a verdict between 'Guilty' or 'Not Guilty'

Question 10

What are the values and principles of the UK based on?

A. European directives

B. History and traditions

C. Norman traditions

D. The reformation of the 18th century

Question 11

Which of these statements is correct?

  A. The period of almost constant warfare after the Norman Conquest up to about AD1485 is called the Middle Ages (or Medieval period).

  B. The period of relative peace after the Norman Conquest up to about AD1485 is called the Elizabethan period.

Question 12

What were most members of the Commonwealth once part of?

  A. The United Nations G77 group

  B. The European Union

  C. The Communist Block

  D. The British Empire

Question 13

Is the statement below True or False?

Islands closely linked with the UK such as the Channel Islands and the Isle of Man are called Crown Dependencies.

Question 14

Which of these statements is correct?

  A. Football is the UK's most popular sport

  B. Rugby the UK's most popular sport.

Question 15

What TWO words are used to refer to everyone in the UK?

  A. British

  B. Britain

  C. Anglo Saxon

  D. Norman

Question 16

Which of these statements is correct?

    A. Towns, cities and rural areas are governed by crown nominated councils.

    B. Towns, cities and rural areas are governed by democratically elected councils.

Question 17

Who were the TWO English and Scottish kings who successfully fought the Vikings?

    A. Alfred the Great

    B. Kenneth MacAlpin

    C. Cnut

    D. Harold

Question 18

Is the statement below True or False?

The UK has developed the Atomic Bomb

Question 19

What is 'the Ashes'?

    A. A series of Test matches played between England and Australia

    B. A famous landscape painting by Joseph Turner (1755-1851)

    C. A novel written by Graham Greene

    D. A First World War poem about the Battle of the Somme written by Wilfred Owen

Question 20

What is the official name of the country?

    A. The United Kingdom of Great Britain

    B. The United Kingdom of Great Britain and Northern Ireland

    C. The United Kingdom

    D. The United Kingdom of Great Britain and Ireland

Question 21

What did Dame Ellen MacArthur achieve in 2004?

    A. The fastest person to sail around the world singlehanded

    B. A gold medal in the 2004 Athens Olympics heptathlon

    C. The youngest member of the British team at the 2004 Athens Olympic games

    D. A gold medal in the javelin at the 2004 Athens Olympics

Question 22

Is the statement below True or False?

Punch was a satirical magazine first published in the 1840s.

Question 23

Which prize have Sir William Golding, Seamus Heaney and Harold Pinter all won?

    A. The Turner Prize

    B. The Nobel Prize for literature

    C. The Mercury Prize

    D. An Oscar for best supporting actor

Question 24

Which of these statements is correct?

    A. Members of the European Parliament are called MEPs.

    B. Members of the Council of Europe are called MEPs.

Practice Test 3 – Answers

Question 1 - False

Question 2 - B

Question 3 - A & C

Question 4 - B

Question 5 - B

Question 6 - True

Question 7 - A

Question 8 - D

Question 9 - False

Question 10 - B

Question 11 - A

Question 12 - D

Question 13 - True

Question 14 - A

Question 15 - A & B

Question 16 - B

Question 17 - A & B

Question 18 - True

Question 19 - A

Question 20 - B

Question 21 - A

Question 22 - True

Question 23 - B

Question 24 - A

PRACTICE TEST 4

Question 1

The invasion of which country Germany in 1939 prompted Britain to go to war?

A. Czechoslovakia

B. Belgium

C. Poland

D. France

Question 2

Which of these statements is correct?

A. London has 33 local authorities.

B. London has 55 local authorities.

Question 3

Is the statement below True or False?

George and Robert Stephenson pioneered the railway engine.

Question 4

What is the largest banknote denomination in the UK?

A. £20

B. £40

C. £50

D. £100

Question 5

Which of these statements is correct?

A. The UK is a Parliamentary Democracy with the monarch as head of state.

B. The UK is a Parliamentary Dictatorship with the monarch as head of state.

Question 6

Is the statement below True or False?

The public are not allowed into the Houses of Parliament and House of Commons .

Question 7

What was the symbol of the House of Tudor?

    A. A red rose with a white rose inside it

    B. A boar with a crescent

    C. A fleur de-lis and a falcon

    D. Three lions

Question 8

Which TWO groups cannot stand for public office?

    A. UK citizens aged 18 or over

    B. Members of the armed forces

    C. Civil servants

    D. Commonwealth citizens aged 18 or over

Question 9

Which TWO pieces of classical music did George Frederick Handel compose?

    A. Messiah

    B. Land of Hope and Glory

    C. Billy Bud

    D. Water Music

Question 10

Is the statement below True or False?

The population in the UK in 2010 was just over 30 million.

Question 11

Which of these statements is correct?

    A. Howard Florey discovered penicillin in 1928 which was then developed into a usable drug by Alexander Fleming and Ernst Chain.

    B. Alexander Fleming discovered penicillin in 1928 which was then developed into a usable drug by Howard Florey and Ernst Chain.

Question 12

Which of these statements is correct?

    A. 'The Blitz Spirit' is a phrase used to describe Britons pulling together in the face of adversity.

    B. 'The Somme Spirit' is a phrase used to describe Britons pulling together in the face of adversity.

Question 13

If you have debts what legal action might be taken against you?

    A. You might be taken to court

    B. You could be imprisoned

    C. You could be prosecuted for a criminal offence

    D. All your assets could be confiscated

Question 14

Which of these statements is correct?

    A. Charles (Charlie) Chaplin became famous in silent movies for his tramp character.

    B. David Cameron became famous in silent movies for his tramp character.

Question 15

Which TWO of Henry VIII's six wives were executed?

    A. Jane Seymour

    B. Ann Boleyn

    C. Catherine Howard

    D. Anne of Cleves

Question 16

Which of these statements is correct?

    A. Islands closely linked with the UK such as the Channel Islands and the Isle of Man are called Crown Dependencies.

    B. Islands closely linked with the UK such as the Channel Islands and the Isle of Man are called Overseas Territories.

Question 17

Is the statement below True or False?

The most important minister in Parliament became known as the Chancellor of the Exchequer.

Question 18

What TWO things do we know about the Black Death which came to Britain in 1348?

    A. It was probably a form of plague

    B. It was always fatal

    C. One third of the population of England died

    D. It was spread by cats and dogs

Question 19

Is the statement below True or False?

The UK is governed by the parliament sitting in Westminster.

Question 20

What is the capital city of the UK?

    A. Edinburgh

    B. Cardiff

    C. London

    D. Belfast

Question 21

The aim of which organization is "to prevent war and promote international peace and security"?

    A. The United Nations

    B. The Commonwealth

    C. NATO

    D. The European Union

Question 22

What TWO things must you have in order to become a permanent resident or citizen of the UK?

    A. A good understanding of Life in the UK

    B. Have passed the UK Test

    C. Be married to a British citizen

    D. Have been resident in the UK for 1 year

Question 23

Is the statement below True or False?

Morecambe and Wise were music hall comedians who went on the become stars of television.

Question 24

Name the TWO leading fashion designers below?

    A. Jessica Ennis

    B. Mary Quant

    C. Vivienne Westwood

    D. Jane Grey

Practice Test 4 – Answers

Question 1 - C

Question 2 - A

Question 3 - True

Question 4 - C

Question 5 - A

Question 6 - False

Question 7 - A

Question 8 - B & C

Question 9 - A & D

Question 10 - False

Question 11 - B

Question 12 - A

Question 13 - A

Question 14 - A

Question 15 - B & C

Question 16 - A

Question 17 - False

Question 18 - A & C

Question 19 - True

Question 20 - C

Question 21 - A

Question 22 - A & B

Question 23 - True

Question 24 - B & C

PRACTICE TEST 5

Question 1

Who led the last successful foreign invasion of England?

    A. James IV of Scotland

    B. William the Conqueror (the Duke of Normandy)

    C. Isabella of France and Roger Mortimer

    D. Lambert Simnel

Question 2

Is the statement below True or False?

Alan Turing is a famous scientist who showed how gravity applied to the whole universe.

Question 3

Is the statement below True or False?

After the Black Death there were labour shortages and peasants began to demand higher wages.

Question 4

Which of these statements is correct?

    A. Individuals rights and individual freedoms have their roots in Magna Carta, the Habeas Corpus Act and the Bill of Rights of 1680.

    B. Individuals rights and individual freedoms have their roots in The Human Rights Act.

Question 5

What TWO social changes did the Black Death lead to?

    A. New social classes appeared

    B. People left the countryside to live in the towns

    C. People left the UK to go and make new lives in Europe

    D. Women gained the right to keep their property after getting married

Question 6

Is the statement below True or False?

Joseph Turner was an influential landscape painter.

Question 7

Which of these statements is correct?

A. The Falkland Islands and St Helena are Crown Dependencies linked to the UK but not part of it.

B. The Falkland Islands and St Helena are Overseas Territories linked to the UK but not part of it.

Question 8

Is the statement below True or False?

The spiritual leader of the Church of England is the monarch.

Question 9

Which of these statements is correct?

A. Acts of Parliament in 1872 and 1882 gave women the right to keep their own earnings and property.

B. Acts of Parliament in 1872 and 1882 gave women the right to vote.

Question 10

Is the statement below True or False?

Edward 1 built huge castles, including Conwy and Caernarvon, in Wales to maintain his power.

Question 11

Which of these statements is correct?

A. The Eden project in Cornwall is a charity which runs environmental and social projects internationally.

B. The Eden project in Suffolk is a a charity which runs prison offender rehabilitation programmes.

Question 12

What is not a job of the police?

    A. To protect life and property

    B. To prevent disturbances

    C. To prevent and detect crime

    D. To prevent immigration

Question 13

How is the UK governed?

    A. By Parliament sitting in Westminster

    B. By the European Parliament sitting in Strasbourg

    C. By the Privy Council sitting in Westminster

    D. By the monarch and their advisers

Question 14

Which of these statements is correct?

    A. The First World War ended at 11.00am on 11 November 1918 with victory for Britain and its allies.

    B. The First World War ended 8 May 1945 with victory for Britain and its allies.

Question 15

Which charter of rights established that even the king was subject to law in 1215?

    A. Magna Carta

    B. Charter of the Forest

    C. King John's Charter

    D. The Baron's Charter

Question 16

What is the role of judges?

    A. To interpret the law and to ensure that trials are conducted fairly

    B. To decide whether someone is guilty of a crime or offence

    C. To recommend new laws and regulations

    D. To decide whether there is enough evidence to prosecute someone.

Question 17

What were TWO names of the opposing groups in the English civil war?

    A. Jacobites

    B. Picts

    C. Roundheads

    D. Cavaliers

Question 18

Which of these statements is correct?

    A. Every year there is a popular rowing race on the river Severn between Oxford and Cambridge universities.

    B. Every year there is a popular rowing race on the river Thames between Oxford and Cambridge universities.

Question 19

What language other than English is spoken in Scotland?

    A. Manx

    B. Guernésiais

    C. Sercquiais

    D. Gaelic

Question 20

Which TWO of these were well known landscape gardeners?

    A. Lancelot 'Capability' Brown

    B. Clarice Cliff

    C. Gertrude Jekyll

    D. Thomas Chippendale

Question 21

Historically, what religion is the UK?

    A. Muslim

    B. Buddhist

    C. Atheist

    D. Christian

Question 22

Which TWO battles was Charles II defeated at when he invaded England with a Scottish army?

    A. Dunbar

    B. Worcester

    C. Marston Moor

    D. Hastings

Question 23

Identify two of the principles included in the European Convention on Human rights, below

    A. Right to life

    B. Prohibition of torture

    C. Right to freedom of movement

    D. Prohibition of corruption

Question 24

Is the statement below True or False?

The UK is one of five permanent members of the UN Security Council.

Practice Test 5 – Answers

Question 1 - B

Question 2 - False

Question 3 - True

Question 4 - A

Question 5 - A & B

Question 6 - True

Question 7 - B

Question 8 - False

Question 9 - A

Question 10 - True

Question 11 - A

Question 12 - D

Question 13 - A

Question 14 - A

Question 15 - A

Question 16 - A

Question 17 - C & D

Question 18 - B

Question 19 - D

Question 20 - A & C

Question 21 - D

Question 22 - A & B

Question 23 - A & B

Question 24 - True

PRACTICE TEST 6

Question 1

Is the statement below True or False?

The UK is made up of England, Scotland and Wales.

Question 2

Who wrote a series of poems in English about a group of people going to Canterbury on a pilgrimage in around 1400?

    A. William Blake

    B. Graham Greene

    C. Roger Mortimer

    D. Geoffrey Chaucer

Question 3

Name TWO events of the reign of Elizabeth I

    A. The Spanish Armada

    B. The Jacobite rebellion

    C. The execution of Mary Queen of Scots

    D. The War of the Roses

Question 4

Is the statement below True or False?

Captain Francis Drake mapped the coast of Australia.

Question 5

Which TWO countries are not parts of 'Great Britain'?

    A. England

    B. Wales

    C. Northern Ireland

    D. Ireland

Question 6

Is the statement below True or False?

To be able to vote in a parliamentary, local or European election you must be on the electoral register.

Question 7

Which of these statements is correct?

    A.   Stonehenge is a Stone Age monument found in the English County of Wiltshire.

    B.   Maiden Castle is a Stone Age fortification found in the English County of Wiltshire.

Question 8

Is the statement below True or False?

The rose is associated with the country of England

Question 9

What is the official Church of the state?

    A.   The Methodist Church

    B.   The Catholic Church

    C.   The Church of England

    D.   The Church of the UK

Question 10

Where are most criminal cases dealt with in England, Wales and Northern Ireland?

    A.   Magistrates Court

    B.   County Court

    C.   High Court

    D.   Sheriff Court

Question 11

Which of these statements is correct?

   A. In 1997 the Labour government led by Edward Heath was elected.

   B. In 1997 the Labour government led by Tony Blair was elected.

Question 12

Which of these statements is correct?

   A. Major sporting stadiums include Wembley Stadium, London and the Millennium Stadium in Cardiff.

   B. Major sporting stadiums include the Millennium Dome, London and Aintree, Merseyside.

Question 13

Which of these statements is correct?

   A. Diwali falls in October or November and is celebrated by Muslims.

   B. Diwali falls in October or November and is celebrated by Hindus and Sikhs.

Question 14

Which of these statements is correct?

   A. A District Judge chairs debates in the House of Commons.

   B. The Speaker chairs debates in the House of Commons.

Question 15

At what TWO occasions is the national anthem played?

   A. In cinemas before the film show starts

   B. When British TV stations close down for the night

   C. At important national occasions

   D. At events attended by the Queen

Question 16

Which is not a devolved parliament or assembly?

    A. The Scottish Parliament

    B. The Welsh Assembly

    C. The Northern Ireland Assembly

    D. The English Parliament

Question 17

Is the statement below True or False?

Julius Caesar led an unsuccessful Roman invasion of Britain in 55BC.

Question 18

What TWO things did Edward I of England do in 1284?

    A. Introduced the Statute of Rhuddlan

    B. Annexed Wales to the Crown

    C. Defeated the Scots at the Battle of Culloden

    D. Signed Magna Carta

Question 19

Is the statement below True or False?

The Dame is a man played by a woman in pantomimes.

Question 20

Which king is most famous for breaking from the Church of Rome and marrying six times?

    A. Henry VIII

    B. Edward I

    C. Charles II

    D. George III

Question 21

Which of these statements is correct?

    A. In 1969 the voting age was reduced to 18 for men and women.

    B. In 1969 the voting age was reduced to 16 for men and women.

Question 22

By what name is 1 April known when people play jokes on each other until midday?

    A. April Fool's Day

    B. April Joke Day

    C. Trick or Treat Day

    D. Jollity Day

Question 23

How long can you use a driving licence from a non-EU country in the UK?

    A. For up to 6 months

    B. For up to 12 months

    C. For up to 5 years

    D. Until you are 70 years old

Question 24

Which TWO countries were part of the Axis powers in the Second World War?

    A. Italy

    B. France

    C. Japan

    D. Russia

Practice Test 6 – Answers

Question 1 - False
Question 2 - D

Question 3 - A & C

Question 4 - False

Question 5 - C & D

Question 6 - True

Question 7 - A

Question 8 - True

Question 9 - C

Question 10 - A

Question 11 - B

Question 12 - A

Question 13 - B

Question 14 - B

Question 15 - C & D

Question 16 - D

Question 17 - True

Question 18 - A & B

Question 19 - False

Question 20 - A

Question 21 - A

Question 22 - A

Question 23 - B

Question 24 - A & C

PRACTICE TEST 7

Question 1

Is the statement below True or False?

There are 15 national parks in England, Wales and Scotland.

Question 2

Which is a responsibility and freedom not shared by all those living in the UK?

    A. Respect and obey the law

    B. Treat others with fairness

    C. Respect and obey the monarch

    D. Look after yourself and your family

Question 3

Is the statement below True or False?

The UK is a Parliamentary Dictatorship with the monarch as head of state.

Question 4

Which of these statements is correct?

    A. Catherine Howard who married Henry VIII was accused of taking lovers and executed.

    B. Catherine of Aragon, first wife of Henry VIII, was accused of taking lovers and executed.

Question 5

In 1560 what did the predominantly Protestant Scottish Parliament abolish?

    A. The right to carry swords

    B. The authority of the Pope

    C. Clandestine marriages

    D. The right of Protestants to attend church

Question 6

Which of these statements is correct?

    A. The capital city of Wales is Cardiff

    B. The capital city of Wales is Swansea

Question 7

Which of these statements is correct?

    A. Andy Murray is a Scottish tennis player who is the first British man to win a singles title in a Grand Slam tournament since 1936.

    B. David Lloyd is a Scottish tennis player who is the first British man to win a singles title in a Grand Slam tournament since 1936.

Question 8

Is the statement below True or False?

'Great Britain' refers only to England and Scotland.

Question 9

Which of these statements is correct?

    A. Members of the House of Lords, known as peers, are not elected and do not represent a constituency.

    B. Members of the House of Commons, known as MPs, are not elected and do not represent a constituency.

Question 10

Is the statement below True or False?

Robert Adam designed palaces such as Hampton Court in England.

Question 11

Which TWO flowers are national flowers for countries within the UK?

    A. Rose

    B. Lilly

    C. Iris

    D. Thistle

Question 12

Which of these statements is correct?

    A. Missionaries converted the Anglo-Saxons to Christianity.

    B. The Normans converted the Anglo-Saxons to Christianity.

Question 13

Is the statement below True or False?

King Philip of Spain was defeated by the Duke of Wellington (The Iron Duke) at the Battle of Waterloo.

Question 14

Why doesn't the Welsh dragon appear on the first Union Jack created in 1606?

    A. Because Queen Victoria thought the dragon symbol was unlucky

    B. Because, at that time, Wales was in rebellion against England

    C. Because the Welsh voted not to include it in a referendum

    D. Because the Principality of Wales was already united with England

Question 15

Is the statement below True or False?

In the middle of the 19th century Ireland suffered a famine and a million people died when the potato crop failed.

Question 16

To whom was Winston Churchill referring in his speech with the words 'Never in the field of human conflict was so much owed by so many to so few'

    A. Royal Air Force pilots during the Battle of Britain

    B. Royal Navy officers following the evacuation of Dunkirk

    C. 8th Army soldiers following the victory of El Alamein

    D. British soldiers shortly after the successful D-day landings

Question 17

The third Sunday in June is known by which other name?

    A. Mother's Day

    B. St Patrick's Day

    C. Father's day

    D. Hanukkah

Question 18

Which TWO of these are not Christian festivals?

    A. Diwali

    B. Lent

    C. Valentine's Day

    D. Shrove Tuesday

Question 19

The work of which German refugee, at Stoke Mandeville hospital became the origin of the Paralympic games?

    E. Ludwig Guttmann

    F. Lucian Freud

    G. Daniel Marot

    H. Michael Marks

Question 20

Where do residents of the UK have to register their car or motorcycle?

    A. With the Driver and Vehicle Licensing Agency (DVLA)

    B. With the Department for Transport (DoT)

    C. With the Automobile Association (AA)

    D. With the Highways Agency (HA)

Question 21

What can you be randomly selected for if you are on the electoral register and between the ages of 18 and 70?

    A. Jury Service

    B. The Army

    C. Community Service

    D. Charity Service

Question 22

Why did Charles I enter the House of Commons?

    A. To present his case to the members of parliament

    B. To dissolve parliament

    C. To try to arrest five parliamentary leaders

    D. To arrest the Speaker

Question 23

In which TWO ways can you gain entry to the UK Parliament?

    A. Write to your local MP

    B. Queue on the day at the public entrance

    C. Order online

    D. Collect from the Citizens Advice Bureau

Question 24

What is British society founded upon?

    A. The monarchy

    B. Fundamental values and principles

    C. The legislation passed by Parliament

    D. European directives and legislation

Practice Test 7 – Answers

Question 1 - True

Question 2 - C

Question 3 - False

Question 4 - A

Question 5 - B

Question 6 - A

Question 7 - A

Question 8 - False

Question 9 - A

Question 10 - False

Question 11 - A & D

Question 12 - A

Question 13 - False

Question 14 - D

Question 15 - True

Question 16 - A

Question 17 - C

Question 18 - A & D

Question 19 - A

Question 20 - A

Question 21 - A

Question 22 - C

Question 23 - A & B

Question 24 - B

PRACTICE TEST 8

Question 1

What are TWO of the changes that the Chartists called for?

    A. Secret ballots

    B. Legalisation of gay marriage

    C. MPs to be paid

    D. An exit of the European Union

Question 2

Is the statement below True or False?

When Queen Anne died in 1714, Parliament chose a German, George I to be the next king because he was Anne's nearest Protestant relative.

Question 3

Is the statement below True or False?

Oliver Cromwell and his son Richard both believed in the 'Divine Right of Kings'.

Question 4

What insurance must you have if you drive a car?

    A. Public liability insurance

    B. Personal liability insurance

    C. Accidental damage insurance

    D. Motor insurance

Question 5

What does the Habeaus Corpus Act of 1679 state?

    A. That every prisoner has a right to a court hearing

    B. That acts of treason were punishable by death

    C. That people could be tortured if they refused to go to trial before a jury

    D. That women would keep their property and wealth when they got married

Question 6

Is the statement below True or False?

If you are employed your employer typically deducts income tax through a system called PAYE.

Question 7

Select TWO famous British films from the list below

    A. Touching the Void

    B. Alien

    C. Saving Private Ryan

    D. Lawrence of Arabia

Question 8

Which of these statements is correct?

    A. John Major was Prime Minister after Margaret Thatcher and helped establish the Northern Ireland peace process

    B. Gordon Brown was Prime Minister after Margaret Thatcher and helped establish the Northern Ireland peace process

Question 9

Is the statement below True or False?

Islands closely linked with the UK such as the Channel Islands and the Isle of Man are called Overseas Territories.

Question 10

What TWO things was the Reformation a move against?

    A. The 'divine right of kings'

    B. The ideas and practices of the Monarchy

    C. The authority of the pope

    D. The ideas and practices of the Roman Catholic Church

Question 11

Is the statement below True or False?

The day before Easter starts is called Shrove Tuesday or Pancake Day.

Question 12

How do new citizens show that they will uphold the values of the UK at the citizenship ceremony?

    A. They take a pledge

    B. They sign a charter

    C. They sign a register

    D. They make a donation

Question 13

Which of these statements is correct?

    A. The Giant's Causeway on the north-east coast of Wales is a land formation of columns made from volcanic lava.

    B. The Giant's Causeway on the north-east coast of Northern Ireland is a land formation of columns made from volcanic lava.

Question 14

How old do you have to be before you can become a school governor?

    A. 18 or over

    B. 21 or over

    C. 30 or over

    D. 40 or over

Question 15

Which of these statements is correct?

    A. At 16 people can drink wine or beer with a meal in a hotel or restaurant as long as they are with someone over 18.

    B. At 14 people can drink wine or beer with a meal in a hotel or restaurant as long as they are with someone over 18.

Question 16

Which of these statements is correct?

A. School Governors must be aged 30 or over on the date of their election or appointment.

B. School Governors must be aged 18 or over on the date of their election or appointment.

Question 17

Who succeeded Oliver Cromwell as Lord Protector?

A. His brother Henry Cromwell

B. His son Richard Cromwell

C. His cousin James Cromwell

D. His daughter Elizabeth Cromwell

Question 18

Which of these statements is correct?

A. Drivers can use their driving licence until they are 70 years old.

B. Drivers can use their driving licence until they are 65 years old.

Question 19

What were the TWO main groups in the houses of Parliament at the time of the Restoration?

A. Labour

B. Whigs

C. Tories

D. Liberals

Question 20

Which of these statements is correct?

A. In 1982, Argentina invaded the Falkland Islands, a British Overseas Territory and military action led to the recovery of the islands (The Falklands War).

B. In 1982, Argentina invaded the Faroe Islands, a British Overseas Territory and military action led to the recovery of the islands (The Faroes War).

Question 21

Where did cricket originate?

    A. Scotland

    B. Wales

    C. England

    D. Ireland

Question 22

What TWO things are true about the Life in the UK test?

    A. The test consists of 24 questions

    B. You have 35 minutes to pass the test

    C. There are about 100 test centres around the UK

    D. You need to take some identification and proof of address with you to the test

Question 23

Who captained the English football team that won the World Cup in 1966?

    A. Bobby Moore

    B. Gordon Banks

    C. Norman Hunter

    D. Jimmy Greaves

Question 24

Is the statement below True or False?

William Wordsworth wrote poems inspired by nature.

Practice Test 8 – Answers

Question 1 - A & C

Question 2 - True

Question 3 - False

Question 4 - D

Question 5 - A

Question 6 - True

Question 7 - A & D

Question 8 - A

Question 9 - False

Question 10 - C & D

Question 11 - True

Question 12 - A

Question 13 - B

Question 14 - A

Question 15 - A

Question 16 - B

Question 17 - B

Question 18 - A

Question 19 - B & C

Question 20 - A

Question 21 - C

Question 22 - A & D

Question 23 - A

Question 24 - True

PRACTICE TEST 9

Question 1

Is the statement below True or False?

The UK is governed by the parliament sitting in Holyrood

Question 2

Which of these statements is correct?

A. King Richard III of the House of York was killed in the Battle of Bosworth Field.

B. James IV of Scotland was killed in the Battle of Bosworth Field.

Question 3

What TWO things do we know about Sir Francis Drake?

A. He discovered the potato and tobacco

B. He mapped the coast of Australia

C. He was one of the commanders in the defeat of the Spanish Armada

D. His ship The Golden Hind was one of the first to sail right around the world

Question 4

What does 'Great Britain' refer to?

A. England, Scotland, Wales and Northern Ireland

B. England and Wales

C. England, Scotland and Wales

D. England and Scotland

Question 5

Is the statement below True or False?

The laws passed after the Wars of the Roses are the beginning of what is called a 'constitutional monarchy'.

Question 6

Who is the first British man to win a Grand Slam tennis tournament since 1936?

A. Andy Murray

B. David Lloyd

C. Tim Henman

D. Roger Taylor

Question 7

Which of these statements is correct?

A. Boxing day is the day before Christmas day.

B. Boxing day is the day after Christmas day.

Question 8

Which TWO of these were well known architects?

A. Inigo Jones

B. Robert Adam

C. Dylan Thomas

D. William Beveridge

Question 9

Which of these statements is correct?

A. Bobby Moore captained the English Football team that won the World Cup in 1966.

B. Jacky Charlton captained the English Football team that won the World Cup in 1966.

Question 10

Which of these statements is correct?

A. The Queen is the ceremonial head of the Council of Europe.

B. The Queen is the ceremonial head of the Commonwealth.

Question 11

Is the statement below True or False?

You need to be at least 16 years old to ride a moped on public roads.

Question 12

Which famous scientist born in 1643 discovered that white light is made up of the colours of the rainbow?

A. Max Planck

B. Blaise Pascal

C. Isaac Newton

D. Caroline Herschel

Question 13

Which of these statements is correct?

A. Edward VI established the Book of Common Prayer for the Church of England.

B. James I established the Book of Common Prayer for the Church of England.

Question 14

How was William of Orange, the Protestant ruler of the Netherlands related to James II?

A. He was his brother

B. He was married to James II's elder daughter

C. There was no family connection

D. He was his uncle

Question 15

What memorial is the centrepiece of the Remembrance Day service in the UK?

A. Nelson's Column, in Trafalgar Square

B. Monument, in the City of London

C. The Cenotaph, in Whitehall, London

D. The Scott Monument, Edinburgh

Question 16

Is the statement below True or False?

In Scotland 31 December is called Hogmanay

Question 17

Who could vote at the turn of the 19th century?

A. Men and women over 21 years of age
B. Men who were over 21 years of age and who owned a certain amount of
C. Men who were over 18 years of age and who owned a certain amount of property
D. Men and women over 18 years of age

Question 18

Is the statement below True or False?

'The Restoration' is a period in the 18th century when new ideas about politics, philosophy and science were developed.

Question 19

What are the TWO types of law in the UK?

A. Consolidated
B. Criminal
C. Civil
D. Crown

Question 20

When was the voting age for men and women reduced to 18?

A. 1918
B. 1928
C. 1939
D. 1969

Question 21

Where was the Great Exhibition of 1851 held?

A. Buckingham Palace

B. Blenheim Palace

C. Crystal Palace

D. Alexander Palace

Question 22

Which of these statements is correct?

A. You can write to your MP for free tickets to the Houses of Parliament and House of Commons.

B. You can write to your MP to purchase tickets to the Houses of Parliament and House of Commons.

Question 23

Select the TWO plays by William Shakespeare from the list below

A. Hamlet

B. Far from the Madding Crowd

C. Lucky Jim

D. Macbeth

Question 24

What TWO types of electoral system can be found in use in the UK and its devolved administrations?

A. First past the post

B. Proportional representation

C. Alternative vote

D. Alternative vote plus

Practice Test 9 – Answers

Question 1 - False

Question 2 - A

Question 3 - C & D

Question 4 - C

Question 5 - False

Question 6 - A

Question 7 - B

Question 8 - A & B

Question 9 - A

Question 10 - B

Question 11 - True

Question 12 - C

Question 13 - A

Question 14 - B

Question 15 - C

Question 16 - False

Question 17 - B

Question 18 - False

Question 19 - B & C

Question 20 - D

Question 21 - C

Question 22 - A

Question 23 - A & D

Question 24 - A & B

PRACTICE TEST 10

Question 1

Name TWO of the comic operas written by Gilbert and Sullivan

A. Jesus Christ Superstar

B. Romeo and Juliet

C. HMS Pinafore

D. The Mikado

Question 2

Is the statement below True or False?

All dogs in public places must wear a collar showing the name and address of the owner

Question 3

What is the first line of the national anthem?

A. And did those feet in ancient time

B. God save our gracious Queen

C. I vow to thee, my country

D. Land of Hope and Glory

Question 4

Who is the famous Scottish poet (who wrote in the Scots language, English with some Scottish words and standard English)?

A. John Galt

B. Robert Burns

C. Walter Scott

D. George MacDonald

Question 5

Which of these statements is correct?

A. The inventor of the World Wide Web, Sir Frank Whittle was born in Northern Ireland.

B. The inventor of the World Wide Web, Sir Tim Berners-Lee is British.

Question 6

In what TWO ways can you help the environment?

A. Walk or use public transport

B. Use your car to drive to work

C. Shop for international products

D. Recycle as much of your waste as you can

Question 7

Where did Rugby originate?

A. France

B. England

C. Wales

D. Scotland

Question 8

Which of these statements is correct?

A. April Fool's Day, 1 April is a day when people play jokes on each other until midday.

B. Diwali, 1 April is a day when people play jokes on each other until midday.

Question 9

Which of these statements is correct?

A. The Turner Prize celebrates contemporary art

B. The Turner Prize celebrates works of fiction

Question 10

What did Charles Stuart Parnell mean when he advocated 'Home Rule' for Ireland?

    A. That Ireland would remain in the UK but have its own parliament

    B. That Ireland would be completely independent and ruled from Dublin

    C. That Ireland would be partitioned with Northern Ireland ruled from London

    D. That Northern Ireland would be completely independent and ruled from Belfast

Question 11

Is the statement below True or False?

You have to be 18 or more to participate in the National Lottery

Question 12

Which of these statements is correct?

    A. The Chancellor of the Exchequer is responsible for the Economy

    B. The Minister of Finance is responsible for the Economy

Question 13

Is the statement below True or False?

Female genital mutilation (FGM) also known as cutting or female circumcision is illegal in the UK

Question 14

Which TWO of these are notable authors and writers?

    A. James Callaghan

    B. Isaac Newton

    C. Jane Austen

    D. Sir Arthur Conan Doyle

Question 15

Which of these statements is correct?

    A. A Northern Ireland Assembly was established after the Belfast Agreement in 1998.

    B. A Northern Ireland Parliament was established after the Dublin Agreement in 1998.

Question 16

Is the statement below True or False?

The Falkland Islands and St Helena are Crown Dependencies linked to the UK but not part of it

Question 17

Who mapped the coast of Australia?

    A. Sir Francis Drake

    B. Captain James Cook

    C. Horatio Nelson

    D. Francis Chichester

Question 18

Which of these statements is correct?

    A. From 1853-1856 Britain fought with Turkey and France against Russia in the Crimean War

    B. From 1853-1856 Britain fought with Turkey and France against Russia in the Boer War

Question 19

Where is Europe's longest dry ski slope?

    A. Tamworth

    B. Edinburgh

    C. Aviemore

    D. London

Question 20

What sort of monarchy does the UK have?

    A. An absolute monarchy

    B. A dependent monarchy

    C. A constitutional monarchy

    D. A republican monarchy

Question 21

Is the statement below True or False?

The people of the Iron Age made the first coins to be minted in Britain.

Question 22

Which TWO developments are associated with the 'Swinging Sixties'?

    A. Children's rights reform

    B. Abortion law reform

    C. Divorce law reform

    D. Decimal currency

Question 23

What TWO things do we know about Mary Queen of Scots?

    A. She was suspected of involvement in the murder of her husband

    B. She invaded Ireland with the help of the French Army

    C. She spent much of her early childhood in France

    D. She was a protestant

Question 24

Is the statement below True or False?

The Carding process for mass production of steel led to the development of shipbuilding and railways.

Practice Test 10 – Answers

Question 1 - C & D

Question 2 - True

Question 3 - B

Question 4 - B

Question 5 - B

Question 6 - A & D

Question 7 - B

Question 8 - A

Question 9 - A

Question 10 - A

Question 11 - False

Question 12 - A

Question 13 - True

Question 14 - C & D

Question 15 - A

Question 16 - False

Question 17 - B

Question 18 - A

Question 19 - B

Question 20 - C

Question 21 - True

Question 22 - B & C

Question 23 - A & C

Question 24 - False

PRACTICE TEST 11

Question 1
Is the statement below True or False?

Edward 1 built huge castles, including Conwy and Caernarvon, in Wales to maintain his power.

Question 2
What style of music was the late 1970s known for?
- A. Grunge
- B. Disco
- C. Punk
- D. Rock

Question 3
What TWO events did Samuel Pepys write about?
- A. The Industrial Revolution
- B. An outbreak of plague in London in 1666
- C. The Great Fire of London
- D. The abolition of slavery

Question 4
What was established by the Treaty of Rome in 1957?
- A. The Euro
- B. The European Union
- C. The Council of Europe
- D. NATO

Question 5

When did the first farmers arrive in Britain?

    A. During the Iron Age

    B. About 6000 years ago

    C. More than 20,000 years ago

    D. In the 14th century

Question 6

Which TWO of these phrases have their origins with the sport of Cricket?

    A. Rain stopped play

    B. Down to the wire

    C. Batting on a sticky wicket

    D. Heavy hitter

Question 7

Which of these statements is correct?

    A. Henry Purcell, an organist at Westminster Abbey, wrote church music, operas and other pieces.

    B. Sir William Walton, an organist at Westminster Abbey, wrote church music, operas and other pieces.

Question 8

Is the statement below True or False?

St Andrew is the patron saint of Wales and St Andrew's day is 1 March.

Question 9

What TWO wars did many English knights take part in during the Middle Ages?

    A. The Crusades for control of the Holy Land

    B. The Hundred Years War with France

    C. The American War of Independence

    D. The Crimean War

Question 10

Is the statement below True or False?

The police form part of the government.

Question 11

Which of these statements is correct?

    A. The war against Japan ended in August 1945 when the United States dropped atom bombs on the cities of Hiroshima and Nagasaki.

    B. The war against Japan ended in August 1945 when the United States dropped atom bombs on the cities of Tokyo and Osaka.

Question 12

Which of these statements is correct?

    A. The official Church of the state is the Church of the United Kingdom (Anglican church) which is Catholic.

    B. The official Church of the state is the Church of England (Anglican church) which is Protestant.

Question 13

Which of these statements is correct?

    A. The National Trust is a charity which keeps many parts of the countryside and places of interest open.

    B. The British Trust is a charity which keeps many parts of the countryside and places of interest open.

Question 14

Which of these statements is correct?

    A. The local residents decide the hours that a pub or night club is open.

    B. The licensee decides the hours that a pub or night club is open.

Question 15

What are the TWO choices for citizens to swear by at the citizenship ceremony?

    A. Oath of allegiance

    B. Affirmation of allegiance

    C. Declaration of allegiance

    D. Vow of allegiance

Question 16

Who founded the Aldeburgh festival in Suffolk?

    A. John Major

    B. Benjamin Britten

    C. Ian Botham

    D. Jeremy Corbyn

Question 17

Which of these statements is correct?

    A. The Department for Health guarantees a minimum standard of care for all, free at the point of use.

    B. The National Health Service guarantees a minimum standard of care for all, free at the point of use.

Question 18

Is the statement below True or False?

The Wimbledon Championships at the All England Tennis Club are the only 'Grand Slam' event played on grass.

Question 19

What did many English knights take part in as part of an effort by European Christians to gain control of 'The Holy Land'?

    A. The War of the Roses

    B. The Crusades

    C. The Reformation

    D. The Restoration

Question 20

Is the statement below True or False?

The charter of rights called Magna Carta established the idea that even the king was subject to the law.

Question 21

What system of election is used in the European elections?

    A. First Past the Post

    B. A Proportional representation

    C. Alternative Vote

    D. Alternative Vote Plus

Question 22

Which TWO islands are Crown Dependencies?

    A. Isle of Man

    B. Scilly Isles

    C. Channel Islands

    D. St Helena

Question 23

Which Roman emperor led the successful invasion of Britain in AD43?

    A. Trajan

    B. Nero

    C. Claudius

    D. Hadrian

Question 24

Who invented the hovercraft in the 1950s?

    A. Sir Tim Berners-Lee

    B. Sir Christopher Cockerill

    C. Sir Ian Wilmot

    D. Sir Frank Whittle

Practice Test 11 – Answers

Question 1 - True

Question 2 - Correct

Question 3 - B & C

Question 4 - B

Question 5 - B

Question 6 - A & C

Question 7 - A

Question 8 - False

Question 9 - A & B

Question 10 - False

Question 11 - A

Question 12 - B

Question 13 - A

Question 14 - B

Question 15 - A & B

Question 16 - B

Question 17 - B

Question 18 - True

Question 19 - B

Question 20 - True

Question 21 - B

Question 22 - A & C

Question 23 - C

Question 24 - B

PRACTICE TEST 12

Question 1

Is the statement below True or False?

King Harold died at the Battle of Hastings .

Question 2

What TWO things did Isaac Newton discover?

    A.   That gravity applied to the whole universe

    B.   That white light is made up of the colours of the rainbow

    C.   That lightning is electrical

    D.   That tides are caused by the moon

Question 3

Which of these statements is correct?

    A.   Henry VIII, famously had six wives.

    B.   Charles II, famously had six wives.

Question 4

Which of these statements is correct?

    A.   Roald Dahl is an author of children's books such as Charlie and the Chocolate Factory and George's Marvellous Medicine Machine.

    B.   Rudyard Kipling is an author of children's books such as Charlie and the Chocolate Factory and George's Marvellous Medicine Machine.

Question 5

Is the statement below True or False?

Two well-known pop groups of the 60s are '*The Police*' and '*The Stranglers*'.

Question 6

Which TWO of these countries joined the European Economic Community when it was first set up?

    A. Belgium

    B. France

    C. United Kingdom

    D. Croatia

Question 7

Which of these statements is correct?

    A. Henry Moore is an English sculptor and artist.

    B. Henry Moore is an English inventor and scientist.

Question 8

Is the statement below True or False?

Rugby originated in Wales in the early 19th Century

Question 9

Which of these statements is correct?

    A. Civil servants are politically neutral.

    B. Members of the House of Lords are politically neutral.

Question 10

How are the values and principles of the UK protected?

    A. By the armed forces

    B. By the judiciary

    C. By law, customs and expectations

    D. By parliament

Question 11

Is the statement below True or False?

Diwali falls in October or November and is celebrated by Muslims.

Question 12

Which TWO of the cities listed below are in England?

    A. Sheffield

    B. Bristol

    C. Cardiff

    D. Glasgow

Question 13

Which English King led the English army at the Battle of Agincourt in 1415?

    A. George I

    B. Richard III

    C. Henry V

    D. Henry VI

Question 14

Which of these statements is correct?

    A. The shamrock is associated with Northern Ireland

    B. The shamrock is associated with Scotland

Question 15

Which English sculptor and artist (1898-1986) is best known for his large bronze abstract sculptures?

    A. John Constable

    B. John Petts

    C. David Hockney

    D. Henry Moore

Question 16

What is the White Tower in the Tower of London an example of?

  A. A Norman Castle Keep

  B. A Roman Fort

  C. An Iron age fortification

  D. A Round Barrow

Question 17

What does the UN Security Council do?

  A. It works towards shared goals in democracy and development

  B. It creates laws called directives, regulations or framework decisions

  C. It recommends action when there are international crises and threats to peace

  D. It is responsible for promotion and protection of human rights

Question 18

Which type of law is used to settle disputes between individuals or groups?

  A. Civil law

  B. Criminal law

  C. Crown law

  D. Local law

Question 19

Is the statement below True or False?

Arranged marriages where both parties agree to the marriage are not acceptable in the UK.

Question 20

Which TWO islands are British Overseas territories?

  A. Isle of Man

  B. St Helena

  C. Channel Islands

  D. Falkland Islands

Question 21

Which of these statements is correct?

    A. Elections to NATO use a system of proportional representation.

    B. Elections to the European Parliament use a system of proportional representation.

Question 22

In the war of the roses which family was represented by a white rose?

    A. The House of Lancaster

    B. The House of Windsor

    C. The House of York

    D. The House of Anjou

Question 23

Which are the TWO Roman forts?

    A. Housesteads

    B. Harlech

    C. Shrewsbury

    D. Vindolanda

Question 24

What was the Harrier jump jet?

    A. A vertical take- off aircraft that combined jet engines and rotor blades

    B. A jet engine famous for its part in the Korean war

    C. A jet engine fighter aircraft capable of taking off vertically

    D. A supersonic commercial jet airliner

Practice Test 12 – Answers

Question 1 - True

Question 2 - A & B

Question 3 - A

Question 4 - A

Question 5 - False

Question 6 - A & B

Question 7 - A

Question 8 - False

Question 9 - A

Question 10 - C

Question 11 - False

Question 12 - A & C

Question 13 - C

Question 14 - A

Question 15 - D

Question 16 - A

Question 17 - C

Question 18 - A

Question 19 - False

Question 20 - B & D

Question 21 - B

Question 22 - C

Question 23 - A & D

Question 24 - C

PRACTICE TEST 13

Question 1

Is the statement below True or False?

The chairperson of the Church of Scotland is the Moderator and is appointed for one year only.

Question 2

Which annual London even showcases garden design from Britain and around the world?

    A. The Hampton Court flower show

    B. The Chatsworth Flower show

    C. The Chelsea Flower show

    D. The Malvern Autumn show

Question 3

What is Maiden Castle in Dorset an impressive example of?

    A. A Roman fort

    B. A Medieval fort

    C. A Tudor fort

    D. An Iron Age hill fort

Question 4

Which of these statements is correct?

    A. William Beveridge wrote the Beveridge Report which recommended that government should find ways of fighting the five 'Giant Evils' of Want, Disease, Ignorance, Squalor and Idleness.

    B. Thomas Cranmer wrote the Cranmer Report which recommended that government should find ways of fighting the five 'Giant Evils' of Want, Disease, Ignorance, Squalor and Idleness.

Question 5

Which of these statements is correct?

A. In the Middle Ages the principle that judges are independent of the government began to be established.

B. In the 18th Century the principle that judges are independent of the government began to be established.

Question 6

Is the statement below True or False?

The television was invented by Scotsman Christopher Cockerell.

Question 7

Which of these statements is correct?

A. Thomas Chippendale designed landscape gardens in the 18th century.

B. Thomas Chippendale designed furniture in the 18th century.

Question 8

Which of these statements is correct?

A. Roast beef with potatoes, vegetables, and Yorkshire pudding is a traditional English food.

B. Roast beef with potatoes, vegetables, and Yorkshire pudding is a traditional Welsh food.

Question 9

Which TWO Stuart Kings believed in the 'divine right of kings?'

A. James I

B. Charles I

C. George III

D. William IV

Question 10

Which of these statements is correct?

    A. In 1928 women won the right to vote at 21, the same age as men.

    B. In 1918 women won the right to vote at 21, the same age as men.

Question 11

Is the statement below True or False?

The British Constitution is not written down in any single document and is described as 'unwritten'.

Question 12

Which of these statements is correct?

    A. New citizens swear or affirm loyalty to the Queen as part of the citizenship ceremony.

    B. New citizens swear or affirm loyalty to the President of the European Union as part of the citizenship ceremony.

Question 13

What flag symbolized the union between England, Scotland, Wales and Ireland in 1801?

    A. The commonwealth flag

    B. The cross of St George

    C. The union flag or Union Jack

    D. The flag of the European Union

Question 14

What is there no place for in British Society?

    A. Pacifism

    B. Extremism

    C. Protest

    D. Apathy

Question 15

Where was William Shakespeare born?

   A. Walton on Thames

   B. Carlisle

   C. London

   D. Stratford-upon-Avon

Question 16

Is the statement below True or False?

The symbol of the House of Lancaster was a red rose and the symbol of the House of York was a white rose.

Question 17

What TWO things does the driving test assess?

   A. Your knowledge

   B. Your practical skills

   C. Your repair and maintenance skills

   D. Your medical fitness

Question 18

Which Anglo Saxon poem tells of its hero's battles against monsters and is still translated into modern English?

   A. Sir Gwain and the Green Knight

   B. If

   C. Beowulf

   D. The Tyger

Question 19

What do parent-teacher associations do?

   A. Organise events to raise money for extra equipment or out of school activities

   B. Ensure the accountability of schools

   C. Monitor and evaluate school performance

   D. Set the strategic direction of schools

Question 20

Who can vote in the UK?

    A. All UK-born and naturalised adult citizens (with a few exceptions)

    B. All members of the European Union (with a few exceptions)

    C. All UK born citizens

    D. All Commonwealth citizens (with a few exceptions)

Question 21

Is the statement below True or False?

Women in Britain make up about half of the total workforce.

Question 22

Which future queen was a daughter of Henry VIII's wife Catherine of Aragon?

    A. Elizabeth I

    B. Mary

    C. Jane

    D. Anne

Question 23

In which TWO areas were comedians Morecambe and Wise stars?

    A. Music hall

    B. Television

    C. Stand up

    D. Satire

Question 24

Which British male athlete was the first in the world to run a mile in under 4 minutes in 1954?

    A. Linford Christie

    B. Roger Bannister

    C. Eric Liddell

    D. Harold Abrahams

Practice Test 13 – Answers

Question 1 - True

Question 2 - C

Question 3 - D

Question 4 - A

Question 5 - A

Question 6 - False

Question 7 - B

Question 8 - A

Question 9 - A & B

Question 10 - A

Question 11 - True

Question 12 - A

Question 13 - C

Question 14 - B

Question 15 - D

Question 16 - True

Question 17 - A & B

Question 18 - C

Question 19 - A

Question 20 - A

Question 21 - True

Question 22 - B

Question 23 - A & B

Question 24 - B

PRACTICE TEST 14

Question 1

Is the statement below True or False?

Scottish Jacobites attempted to put William Wallace on the throne but were defeated.

Question 2

Is the statement below True or False?

Prince Charles (the Prince of Wales) is heir to the throne.

Question 3

At what age can you apply for a free TV licence?

    A. Aged over 60

    B. Aged over 65

    C. Aged over 70

    D. Aged over 75

Question 4

Which TWO lines are taken from speeches by Winston Churchill?

    A. "I have nothing to offer but blood, toil, tears and sweat"

    B. "It was the best of times; it was the worst of times"

    C. "I have a dream"

    D. "We shall never surrender"

Question 5

Is the statement below True or False?

In the 2009 citizenship survey 70% of people identified themselves as Christian.

Question 6

Is the statement below True or False?

Cromwell ruled until his death in 1658 when his son, Richard, became King Richard IV in his place.

Question 7

Which TWO of these sites are Stone Age?

    A. Stonehenge

    B. Skara Brae

    C. Old Sarum

    D. Housesteads

Question 8

Which of these statements is correct?

    A. When Queen Anne died in 1714, Parliament chose a German, George I to be the next king because he was Anne's nearest Protestant relative.

    B. When Queen Anne died in 1714, Parliament chose a Scotsman, James I to be the next king because he was Anne's nearest Protestant relative.

Question 9

Is the statement below True or False?

Agincourt is one of the famous battles of the 'The Hundred Years War' between England and France.

Question 10

What were the 'great evils' that the 1942 Beveridge report recommended that the government should find ways of fighting?

    A. Sloth, Greed, Gluttony, Pride and Deceit

    B. Want, Disease, Ignorance, Squalor and Idleness

    C. Corruption, Inequality, Discrimination and Ignorance

    D. Want, Corruption, Poverty, Global Warming and Discrimination

Question 11

What is an allotment?

A. A piece of land that people can rent where they can grow fruit and vegetables

B. A place that people can store their goods temporarily

C. A type of social housing for those receiving benefits

D. An allocation of goods to a baron by the king

Question 12

Which of these statements is correct?

A. Cars which are more than 3 years old have to pass a Ministry of Transport (MOT) test every year.

B. Cars which are more than 3 years old have to pass an Environmental test every year.

Question 13

Which of these statements is correct?

A. Crisis and Shelter are charities to do with the homeless.

B. Crisis and Shelter are charities to do with disasters emergency relief aid.

Question 14

What are 'Crown dependencies'?

A. Islands closely linked with the UK but not part of it and which have their own governments

B. The countries such as Wales and Scotland which are now part of the UK

C. Islands far from the UK which were once part of the British Empire

D. Commonwealth countries which include the union jack on their flag

Question 15

Which TWO historic Acts show Britain's long history of respecting individual freedoms?

    A. Habeas Corpus Act

    B. The Freedom Act

    C. The Reform Act

    D. The Bill of Rights

Question 16

Who led the Labour government which was elected after the Second World War?

    A. Winston Churchill

    B. Neville Chamberlain

    C. James Callaghan

    D. Clement Attlee

Question 17

Which of these statements is correct?

    A. The spiritual leader of the Church of England is the monarch

    B. The spiritual leader of the Church of England is the Archbishop of Canterbury

Question 18

Which of these statements is correct?

    A. The Education Act 1944 (The Butler Act) introduced free secondary school education in England and Wales.

    B. The Education Act 1944 (The Butler Act) introduced free primary school education in England and Wales.

Question 19

Which TWO are British Overseas Territories?

    A. Cyprus

    B. Falkland Islands

    C. St Helena

    D. Hawaii

Question 20

Which body has the core values of Integrity, Honesty, Objectivity & Impartiality?

  A. The Civil Service

  B. The Army

  C. The Cabinet

  D. The Monarchy

Question 21

How often does Prime Ministers question time take place?

  A. Once a month when Parliament is sitting

  B. Once a fortnight when Parliament is sitting

  C. Once a week when Parliament is sitting

  D. Twice a week when Parliament is sitting

Question 22

Which of these statements is correct?

  A. The day before Christmas starts is called Shrove Tuesday or Pancake Day.

  B. The day before Easter starts is called Shrove Tuesday or Pancake Day.

Question 23

What are the TWO names that the Church of England is also known by?

  A. The Anglican Church

  B. The Presbyterian Church

  C. The Episcopal Church

  D. The Methodist Church

Question 24

Which former captain of the English cricket team holds a number of English Test cricket records for bowling and batting?

  A. Ian Botham

  B. Mike Bradley

  C. Bob Willis

  D. Phil Tufnell

Practice Test 14 – Answers

Question 1 - False

Question 2 - True

Question 3 - D

Question 4 - A & D

Question 5 - True

Question 6 - False

Question 7 - A & B

Question 8 - A

Question 9 - True

Question 10 - B

Question 11 - A

Question 12 - A

Question 13 - A

Question 14 - A

Question 15 - A & D

Question 16 - D

Question 17 - B

Question 18 - A

Question 19 - B & C

Question 20 - A

Question 21 - C

Question 22 - B

Question 23 - A & C

Question 24 - A

PRACTICE TEST 15

Question 1

What was the name of the supersonic commercial airliner that Britain and France developed in the 1960s?

A. De Havilland Comet

B. Concorde

C. Hawker Siddeley Trident

D. Bristol Type 223

Question 2

Is the statement below True or False?

Mary Queen of Scots was Queen Elizabeth I of England's cousin.

Question 3

Which TWO people were important thinkers of the enlightenment?

A. Walter Raleigh

B. Adam Smith

C. David Hume

D. William Walton

Question 4

Is the statement below True or False?

Composer Gustav Holst wrote The Planets.

Question 5

What TWO things do we know about Emmeline Pankhurst (1858-1928)?

A. She was a suffragette

B. She went on hunger strike

C. She died protesting for Women's rights jumping in front of a horse at The Derby

D. She didn't live to see Women given the right to vote at the age of 21, the same as men

Question 6

Is the statement below True or False?

The National Assembly for Wales has elections every 4 years using the 'first past the post' electoral system.

Question 7

Which of these statements is correct?

    A. The union flag consists of the cross of St George; the cross of St Andrew.

    B. The union flag consists of the cross of St George; the cross of St Andrew and the cross of St Patrick.

Question 8

Which of these statements is correct?

    A. In Scotland the national Church is the Church of Scotland which is Methodist.

    B. In Scotland the national Church is the Church of Scotland which is Presbyterian.

Question 9

What was special about Dolly the sheep?

    A. She was the first successfully cloned mammal

    B. She had a genetic marker that made her nails glow in the dark

    C. She was the last of a breed of sheep called 'Welsh Tanface' which is now extinct

    D. She was a pet owned by Queen Elizabeth I

Question 10

Is the statement below True or False?

Steve Redgrave played an important part in changing the law on slavery.

Question 11

Which of these statements is correct?

A. Employees have their National Insurance Contributions deducted from their pay by their employer.

B. Employees have their National Insurance Contributions deducted from their bank account by direct debit.

Question 12

Which of these statements is correct?

A. To get a driving licence you must pass a driving test which tests both your knowledge and practical skills.

B. To get a driving licence you must be able to demonstrate at least 30 hours of driving lessons with an approved provider and have passed a theory test.

Question 14

Which of these statements is correct?

A. Modern British architects include Sir Norman Foster, Lord (Richard) Rogers and Dame Zaha Hadid.

B. Modern British fashion designers include Sir Norman Foster, Lord (Richard) Rogers and Dame Zaha Hadid.

Question 15

What are the words 'Britain', 'British Isles' and 'British' used to describe?

A. Everyone in the United Kingdom

B. Everyone in the United Kingdom and the Crown Dependencies

C. Everyone in the UK and the Overseas Territories

D. Everyone in Great Britain

Question 16

Is the statement below True or False?

The chartists were a group of women who campaigned for greater women's rights and the right to vote.

Question 17

What TWO things is it illegal to do in relation to Female Genital Mutilation (FGM)

    A. Practice FGM

    B. Take a girl or woman abroad for FGM

    C. Take part in education about FGM

    D. Report those at risk of FGM

Question 18

What did many people argue about the unions in the 1970s?

    A. That they had become too powerful and that their activities were harming the UK.

    B. That union members were not adequately protected from the actions of employers.

    C. That unions had become largely irrelevant to the economy of the UK.

    D. That the government should engage more with unions for the benefit of the UK economy.

Question 19

How old must you be to buy alcohol in a pub or night club?

    A. 16 or over

    B. 17 or over

    C. 18 or over

    D. 21 or over

Question 20

What was the clock tower of the Houses of Parliament named in 2012?

    A. Jane Tower

    B. Elizabeth Tower

    C. Mary Tower

    D. Victoria Tower

Question 21

Which is regarded as the more important of the chambers of Parliament?

    A. The House of Commons

    B. The House of MPs

    C. The House of Lords

    D. The House of Lancaster

Question 22

What is the name given to the 20 senior MPs appointed, by the Prime Minister, to become ministers in charge of departments?

    A. The executive board

    B. The crown council

    C. The cabinet

    D. The privy council

Question 23

What TWO things happened when Queen Anne died in 1714?

    A. Parliament chose a German, George I, to be the next king as he was Anne's nearest Protestant relative.

    B. An attempt to get James II's son on the throne was quickly defeated.

    C. Bonnie Prince Charles led a rebellion in Scotland but was defeated at the Battle of the Boyne.

    D. Parliament chose James II's son (also called James) to be the next king.

Question 24

What TWO things can you expect to find at The Tower of London?

    A. The State Apartments

    B. Yeomen Warders, also known as Beefeaters

    C. The Stone of Scone

    D. The Crown Jewels

Practice Test 15 – Answers

Question 1 - B

Question 2 - True

Question 3 - B & C

Question 4 - True

Question 5 - A & B

Question 6 - False

Question 7 - B

Question 8 - B

Question 9 - A

Question 10 - False

Question 11 - A

Question 12 - A

Question 14 - A

Question 15 - A

Question 16 - False

Question 17 - A & B

Question 18 - A

Question 19 - C

Question 20 - B

Question 21 - A

Question 22 - C

Question 23 - A & B

Question 24 - B & D

PRACTICE TEST 16

Question 1
Which is the largest broadcaster in the world?

    A. Al Jazeera

    B. Sky

    C. BBC

    D. CNN

Question 2
Is the statement below True or False?

In the American War of Independence (1760s) thirteen (13) American colonies declared their independence and defeated the British army.

Question 3
Is the statement below True or False?

Bobby Moore captained the English Football team that won the World Cup in 1966.

Question 4
What are TWO of the roles of the Police?

    A. To protect life and property

    B. To prevent and detect crime

    C. To promote international peace and security

    D. To collect taxes

Question 5
Is the statement below True or False?

Henry Edwards became famous in silent movies for his tramp character.

Question 6

Which TWO of these are notable British artists?

    A. John Constable

    B. Sir John Lavery

    C. Mo Farah

    D. Edward Lutyens

Question 7

Which of these statements is correct?

    A. The Bayeux Tapestry commemorates the Battle of Hastings.

    B. The Bayeux Tapestry commemorates the Battle of Britain.

Question 8

Which countries formed the European Economic Community (EEC) in 1957?

    A. Norway, Finland, Denmark, Sweden, the Netherlands and Belgium

    B. West Germany, France, Belgium, Italy, Luxembourg and the Netherlands

    C. West Germany, East Germany, France, the Netherlands and the UK

    D. UK, West Germany, France, Belgium, Italy, Luxembourg and the Netherlands

Question 9

Which of these statements is correct?

    A. The UK joined the European Economic Community in 1973.

    B. The UK joined the Commonwealth in 1973.

Question 10

Which of these statements is correct?

    A. Famous race horsing events include Royal Ascot, the Grand National and the Scottish Grand National.

    B. Famous racing car events include Royal Ascot, the Grand National and the Scottish Grand National.

Question 11

Who became Britain's first woman Prime Minister in 1979?

  A. Emmeline Pankhurst

  B. Glenda Jackson

  C. Theresa May

  D. Margaret Thatcher

Question 12

Is the statement below True or False?

Rudyard Kipling was born in India and wrote books and poems including *The Jungle Book* and the poem *If*.

Question 13

What evidence of speaking and listening skills do you need in order to apply for British Citizenship?

  A. Acceptable evidence of speaking and listening skills in English at A1 of the Common European Framework of Reference

  B. Acceptable evidence of speaking and listening skills in English at B1 of the Common European Framework of Reference

  C. Acceptable evidence of speaking and listening skills in English at C1 of the Common European Framework of Reference

  D. Acceptable evidence of speaking and listening skills in English at B2 of the Common European Framework of Reference.

Question 14

Which are the TWO British national parks listed below?

  A. Joshua Tree

  B. Snowdonia

  C. Trossachs

  D. Yellowstone

Question 15

Which of these statements is correct?

A. The European Convention on Human Rights was produced by the United Nations.

B. The European Convention on Human Rights was produced by the Council of Europe.

Question 16

Which of these statements is correct?

A. Criminal law relates to crimes and are punished by the courts.

B. Civil law relates to crimes and are punished by the courts.

Question 17

Name the TWO famous missionaries from Ireland who spread Christianity in the north during the Anglo Saxon period?

A. St Patrick

B. St Columba

C. St David

D. St Andrew

Question 18

Which of these statements is correct?

A. Henry VII was the first king of 'The House of Tudor'.

B. Henry VII was the first king of 'The House of Stuart'.

Question 19

Which is the highest mountain in Wales?

A. Ben Nevis

B. Snowdon

C. Red Pike

D. Tryfan

Question 20

What is the second largest party in the House of Commons called?

    A. The opposition

    B. The cross benchers

    C. The checkers

    D. The pretenders

Question 21

When do most local authorities hold local elections for councillors each year?

    A. February

    B. May

    C. July

    D. September

Question 23

Select TWO events linked to the Norman Conquest?

    A. The Battle of Hastings

    B. The Creation of the Bayeux Tapestry

    C. The Battle of Marsden Moor

    D. The Peasant's Revolt

Question 24

Is the statement below True or False?

New Year, 1 January is a public holiday.

Practice Test 16 – Answers

Question 1 - C

Question 2 - True

Question 3 - True

Question 4 - A & B

Question 5 - False

Question 6 - A & B

Question 7 - A

Question 8 - B

Question 9 - A

Question 10 - A

Question 11 - D

Question 12 - True

Question 13 - B

Question 14 - B & C

Question 15 - B

Question 16 - A

Question 17 - A & B

Question 18 - A

Question 19 - B

Question 20 - A

Question 21 - B

Question 23 - A & B

Question 24 - True

PRACTICE TEST 17

Question 1

Is the statement below True or False?

In 1918 women over the age of 30 were given the right to vote.

Question 2

Select the TWO famous British poets from the list below?

    A. Ted Hughes

    B. William Blake

    C. Frank Whittle

    D. Alan Turing

Question 3

Is the statement below True or False?

The monarch is the head of the Church of England.

Question 4

Is the statement below True or False?

Sir Chris Hoy was the first man in the world to run a mile in under four minutes

Question 5

What proportion of the UK's total population live in England?

    A. 26%

    B. 52%

    C. 84%

    D. 93%

Question 6

Which of these statements is correct?

    A. In the late 1960s the government passed new laws to restrict immigration to Britain.

    B. In the late 1960s the government passed new laws making it easier to migrate to Britain.

Question 7

Which of these statements is correct?

    A. The Second World War was fought between the Axis powers and the Allies.

    B. The Second World War was fought between the Non-aligned powers and the Grand Alliance.

Question 8

Where is EU law binding?

    A. In the Eurozone

    B. In the UK and all other EU member states

    C. In EU member states other than the UK

    D. It is not binding

Question 9

Which of these statements is correct?

    A. Proceedings in Parliament are published in *Hansard* and broadcast on television.

    B. Proceedings in Parliament are published in *Punch* and broadcast on television.

Question 10

Which of these statements is correct?

    A. People vote in elections at places called 'Polling stations' or 'Polling places'.

    B. People vote in elections at places called 'Voting stations' or 'Voting places'.

Question 11

Which of these statements is correct?

    A. In Scotland a system called 'the Children's Hearing System' is used to deal with children and young people who have committed an offence.

    B. In Scotland a system called 'the Children's Sentencing System' is used to deal with children and young people who have committed an offence.

Question 12

Is the statement below True or False?

In 1851 the Olympics opened in Hyde Park in the Crystal palace, a huge building made of steel and glass.

Question 13

What countries is the UK made up of?

    A. England, Scotland and Wales

    B. England, Scotland, Wales and Northern Ireland

    C. England, Scotland, Wales and Ireland

    D. England, Scotland, Wales, Northern Ireland, Orkney

Question 14

Who took over as Prime Minister from Tony Blair in 2007?

    A. David Cameron

    B. David Callaghan

    C. Gordon Brown

    D. Aneurin Bevan

Question 15

How many American colonies declared their independence from Britain in 1776?

    A. Five (5)

    B. Thirteen (13)

    C. Twenty one (21)

    D. Fifty one (51)

Question 16

Is the statement below True or False?

In the 19th century both men and women over 21 years of age could vote.

Question 17

Which are TWO reasons why the Industrial Revolution happened?

    A. Development of petrochemicals

    B. Development of machinery

    C. Use of steam power

    D. Development of the motor vehicle

Question 18

Which TWO services are National Insurance Contributions used to pay for?

    A. The Armed Forces

    B. The National Health Service

    C. The State Retirement Pension

    D. The Police

Question 19

30 November is the special day of which Scottish saint?

    A. St Andrew

    B. St David

    C. St George

    D. St Patrick

Question 20

What must your name be on in order to vote?

    A. The Electoral register

    B. Hansard

    C. Yellow Pages

    D. The Local Authority directory of voters

Question 21

Who is the ceremonial head of the Commonwealth?

  A. The Prime Minister of England

  B. The Queen

  C. Queen Victoria

  D. An elected President

Question 22

What social changes happened in the Swinging Sixties?

  A. The position of women in the workplace improved

  B. Gay marriage was legalised

  C. The law was changed so that women could vote at the same age as men

  D. Social laws were liberalised in relation to divorce and abortion

Question 23

What are TWO of the roles of school governors?

  A. Teacher recruitment

  B. Setting the strategic direction of the school

  C. Ensuring accountability

  D. Organising and managing school Ofsted inspections

Question 24

Which of these statements is correct?

  A. Any man who forces a woman to have sex, including a woman's husband, can be charged with rape.

  B. Any man who forces a woman to have sex, including a woman's husband, can be charged with common assault.

Practice Test 17 – Answers

Question 1 - True

Question 2 - A & B

Question 3 - True

Question 4 - False

Question 5 - C

Question 6 - A

Question 7 - A

Question 8 - B

Question 9 - A

Question 10 - A

Question 11 - A

Question 12 - False

Question 13 - B

Question 14 - C

Question 15 - B

Question 16 - False

Question 17 - B & C

Question 18 - B & C

Question 19 - A

Question 20 - A

Question 21 - B

Question 22 - A & D

Question 23 - B & C

Question 24 - A

PRACTICE TEST 18

Question 1

Is the statement below True or False?

During the English Civil War those who supported the king were called 'Roundheads' and those who supported Parliament 'the Cavaliers'.

Question 2

Which famous admiral died at the Battle of Trafalgar in 1805?

    A. David Beatty

    B. Cuthbert Collingwood

    C. Horatio Nelson

    D. Charles Stirling

Question 3

What TWO things did the post war Clement Attlee government introduce?

    A. The Welfare State

    B. The Poll Tax

    C. The National Health Service

    D. Identity Cards

Question 4

Is the statement below True or False?

In Scotland 31 December is called Groundhog Day.

Question 5

Which is not a fundamental principle of the UK?

    A. Democracy

    B. The rule of law

    C. Individual liberty

    D. The right to housing

Question 6

Which of these statements is correct?

    A. The television was invented by Scotsman John Logie Baird.

    B. The television was invented by Scotsman Christopher Cockerell.

Question 7

Which of these statements is correct?

    A. Emperor Napoleon of France was defeated by the Duke of Wellington (The Iron Duke) at the Battle of Waterloo.

    B. King Philip of Spain was defeated by the Duke of Wellington (The Iron Duke) at the Battle of Waterloo.

Question 8

Is the statement below True or False?

Until 1870 when a woman got married all her earnings, property and money automatically belonged to her husband.

Question 9

Which TWO of these countries are not members of the Commonwealth?

    A. France

    B. Jamaica

    C. India

    D. Russia

Question 10

Is the statement below True or False?

The National Anthem of the UK is 'Land of Hope and Glory'.

Question 11

Which of these statements is correct?

    A. The National Citizen Service programme gives 16- and 17-year olds the opportunity to enjoy outdoor activities.

    B. The British Outreach programme gives 16- and 17-year olds the opportunity to enjoy outdoor activities.

Question 12

Which of these statements is correct?

    A. National Insurance contributions are used to pay for state benefits such as the state retirement pension and the National Health Service (NHS).

    B. Income Tax is used to pay for state benefits such as the state retirement pension and the National Health Service (NHS).

Question 13

When is Christmas day?

    A. 25 December

    B. 24 December

    C. 1 January

    D. 25 January

Question 14

Who established the first formal anti-slavery groups in Britain?

    A. The Methodists

    B. The Baptists

    C. The Quakers

    D. The Aristocracy

Question 15

What TWO things is Margaret Thatcher known for?

    A. For the Good Friday Agreement

    B. Being the first woman Prime Minister

    C. As the longest serving Prime Minister of the 20th Century

    D. For introducing the Scottish Parliament and the Welsh Assembly

Question 16

Is the statement below True or False?

Cricket is the UK's most popular sport.

Question 17

Which Scottish racing driver won the Formula I world championships three times?

    A. David Coulthard

    B. Jackie Stewart

    C. Ian Stewart

    D. Allan McNish

Question 18

What does NATO stand for?

    A. North Atlantic Treaty Organization

    B. New Atomic Treaty Organization

    C. North Atlantic Trade Organization

    D. New Antiquities Trading Organization

Question 19

What are the TWO different types of Rugby?

    A. League

    B. Federal

    C. Union

    D. Association

Question 20

What type of offence is it to carry a weapon?

    A. A criminal offence

    B. A civil offence

    C. A military offence

    D. A local offence

Question 21

Which of these statements is correct?

    A. Andrew Lloyd Webber and Tim Rice produced the musicals Jesus Christ Superstar and Evita.

    B. Gilbert and Sullivan produced the musicals Jesus Christ Superstar and Evita.

Question 22

Which of these statements is correct?

    A. Easter takes place in March or April and marks the death of Jesus.

    B. Easter takes place in March or April and marks the birth of Jesus.

Question 23

Which TWO soap operas remain very popular?

    A. Game of Thrones

    B. Dr Who

    C. EastEnders

    D. Coronation Street

Question 24

Which athlete has won 16 Paralympic medals, including 11 gold medals, in races over five Paralympic Games?

    A. Ellie Simmonds

    B. Jayne Torvill

    C. Dame Ellen MacArthur

    D. Baroness Tanni Grey-Thompson

Practice Test 18 – Answers

Question 1 - False

Question 2 - C

Question 3 - A & C

Question 4 - False

Question 5 - D

Question 6 - A

Question 7 - A

Question 8 - True

Question 9 - A & D

Question 10 - False

Question 11 - A

Question 12 - A

Question 13 - A

Question 14 - C

Question 15 - B & C

Question 16 - False

Question 17 - B

Question 18 - A

Question 19 - A & C

Question 20 - A

Question 21 - A

Question 22 - A

Question 23 - C & D

Question 24 - D

PRACTICE TEST 19

Question 1

Is the statement below True or False?

Bonfire Night, 5 November is when people set off fireworks to celebrate the failure of plotters, including Guy Fawkes, to kill the Protestant king with a bomb in the Houses of Parliament.

Question 2

What TWO things are you not allowed to discriminate based upon in the UK?

    A. Age

    B. Height

    C. Sex

    D. Qualifications

Question 3

Which of these statements is correct?

    A. The Roman Army left Britain in AD 410 to defend other parts of the Roman Empire.

    B. The Roman Army was forced to leave Britain in AD 410 after it was defeated by the Anglo Saxons.

Question 4

What TWO things are we told about Queen Victoria?

    A. She became queen at the age of 18

    B. During her reign the middle classes became increasingly significant

    C. She died when she was only 25

    D. During her reign England lost many of her overseas colonies

Question 5

Which of these statements is correct?

    A. The most famous Ruby Union competition is the Six Nations Championship.

    B. The most famous Ruby Union competition is the Challenge Cup.

Question 6

Is the statement below True or False?

The Human Rights Act of 1689 confirmed the rights of Parliament and limits of the kings power.

Question 7

Which of these statements is correct?

    A. The Man Booker Prize for fiction is awarded annually for the best fiction novel written by an author from the Commonwealth.

    B. The Mercury Prize for fiction is awarded annually for the best fiction novel written by an author from the Commonwealth.

Question 8

Which of these statements is correct?

    A. The party with the majority of MPs forms the government.

    B. The party with the most votes forms the government.

Question 9

Which of these statements is correct?

    A. Prince Charles (the Prince of Wales) is heir to the throne.

    B. Prince William (the Duke of Cambridge) is heir to the throne.

Question 10

Which TWO of these are patron saints?

    A. St David

    B. St George

    C. St Augustine

    D. St Columba

Question 11

Which of these statements is correct?

A. In the north people united under Kenneth McAlpin against the Vikings and the term Scotland began to be used to describe that country.

B. In the north people united under Macbeth against the Vikings and the term Scotland began to be used to describe that country.

Question 12

During Charles II's reign, in 1665, what happened?

A. There was a major outbreak of plague in London

B. The Peasant's revolt

C. The Spanish Armada

D. The Jacobite rising

Question 13

Which ice skating pair won a gold for ice dancing at the Olympic games in 1984?

A. Judy Blumberg and Michaell Seibert

B. Jayne Torvill and Christopher Dean

C. Jim Sladky and Judy Schwomeyer

D. Marie-France Dubreuil and Patrice Lauzon

Question 14

Where is the Grand National held?

A. At Aintree

B. At Sandown Park

C. At Chepstow

D. At Kempton Park

Question 15

What is it illegal to do in nearly every enclosed pubic space in the UK?

A. To eat

B. To drink

C. To exercise

D. To smoke

Question 16

Who appoints local Police Chief Constables?

A. The Constituency MP

B. The Home Secretary

C. Police and Crime Commissioners

D. The Local Authority

Question 17

Is the statement below True or False?

The Commonwealth has 54 member states most of which were once part of the British Empire.

Question 18

What TWO things happened after the battle of Culloden of 1745?

A. The clans lost a lot of their power and influence

B. The clans grew in power and influence

C. There was a famine in Scotland

D. Clansmen became tenants who had to pay for the land they used

Question 19

What is the name of the British company which gained control of large parts of India?

A. Hudson's Bay Company

B. Royal African Company

C. East India Company

D. Dutch East India Company (Vereenigde Oost-Indische Compagnie)

Question 20

Is the statement below True or False?

Chief Constables are responsible for interpreting the law and ensuring that trials are conducted fairly.

Question 21

Is the statement below True or False?

Sir Arthur Conan Doyle wrote stories about Sherlock Holmes.

Question 22

What are the TWO objectives of the United Nations?

    A. The protection and promotion of human rights

    B. To prevent war

    C. To promote international peace and security

    D. To help each other if they come under attack

Question 23

What does the UK not offer in return for citizens fulfilling their responsibilities and freedoms?

    A. Freedom of belief and religion

    B. Freedom of speech

    C. Freedom to engage in extremism

    D. Freedom from unfair discrimination

Question 24

Which of these statements is correct?

    A. Mary Peters was an athlete who won an Olympic medal in the pentathlon in 1972.

    B. Mary Peters was suffragette who campaigned for women's rights.

Practice Test 19 – Answers

Question 1 - True

Question 2 - A & C

Question 3 - A

Question 4 - A & B

Question 5 - A

Question 6 - False

Question 7 - A

Question 8 - A

Question 9 - A

Question 10 - A & B

Question 11 - A

Question 12 - A

Question 13 - B

Question 14 - A

Question 15 - D

Question 16 - C

Question 17 - True

Question 18 - A & D

Question 19 - C

Question 20 - False

Question 21 - True

Question 22 - B & C

Question 23 - C

Question 24 - A

PRACTICE TEST 20

Question 1
Is the statement below True or False?

The Normans used a system of land ownership known as feudalism.

Question 2
Is the statement below True or False?

The Roman Army left Britain in AD 410 to defend other parts of the Roman Empire.

Question 3
Which TWO of these are famous British composers?
 A. Sir Francis Chichester
 B. Sir Edward Elgar
 C. Sir William Walton
 D. Sir Tim Berners-Lee

Question 4
Is the statement below True or False?

The Anglo-Saxons kingdoms united under King Alfred the Great to defeat the Vikings.

Question 5
Which of these statements is correct?
 A. The capital city of Northern Ireland is Belfast.
 B. The capital city of Northern Ireland is Dublin.

Question 6
Which of these statements is correct?
 A. St David is the patron saint of Wales and St David's day is 1 March.
 B. St Andrew is the patron saint of Wales and St Andrew's day is 1 March.

Question 7

Which of these statements is correct?

    A. In England, Wales and Northern Ireland a jury has 12 members.

    B. In England, Wales and Northern Ireland a jury has 15 members.

Question 8

Which of these statements is correct?

    A. Complaints about the police can be made to an independent body The Police Complaints Commission.

    B. Complaints about the police can be made to an independent body The Police Internal Affairs division.

Question 9

Is the statement below True or False?

Clarice Cliff designed Art Deco ceramics.

Question 10

What do you need in order to apply to become a permanent resident of the UK?

    A. To have a good job

    B. To speak and read English

    C. To have been resident in the UK for more than 6 years

    D. To have a British ancestor

Question 11

What TWO things can the Northern Ireland Assembly make decisions on?

    A. Tax

    B. Education

    C. Health

    D. Defence

Question 12

Which of these statements is correct?

    A. In 1066 the Normans invaded England led by William the Duke of Normandy.

    B. In 1066 the French invaded England led by Louis of France.

Question 13

Which TWO roles form part of the cabinet?

    A. The Home Secretary

    B. The Ministry for Information

    C. The Secretary of State for War

    D. The Chancellor of the Exchequer

Question 14

Which golf course in Scotland is known as the home of golf?

    A. Muirfield

    B. Royal Dornoch

    C. Trump Turnberry

    D. St Andrews

Question 15

Where was the first tennis club founded in 1872?

    A. Wimbledon

    B. Hampton Court

    C. Henley

    D. Leamington Spa

Question 16

From where does the UK currently face threats of terrorism?

    A. From Chechen separatists

    B. From Al' Qa'ida and Northern Ireland

    C. From Argentina and the Falkland Islands

    D. From FARC and Columbia

Question 17

What must the government do if the judges find their actions to be illegal?

    A. Either change policies or ask Parliament to change the law

    B. Replace the judges who did not agree with the government view

    C. Take the case to the European Court of Human Rights

    D. Ask Parliament to overrule the judge's decision

Question 18

How many members does a jury have in England, Wales and Northern Ireland?

    A. 6 people

    B. 12 people

    C. 15 people

    D. 21 people

Question 19

In addition to the cross of St George, which TWO other crosses make up the Union Jack?

    A. The cross of St Patrick

    B. The cross of St Andrew

    C. The cross of St David

    D. The cross of St Columba

Question 20

What TWO things did the Reform Acts of 1832 and 1867 do?

    A. They gave women the right to vote at the age of 30

    B. They greatly increased the number of people with the right to vote

    C. They reduced the amount of property that people needed to have before they could vote

    D. They gave women the right to vote at the same age as men

Question 21

What TWO works did Rudyard Kipling write?

- A. The daffodils
- B. If
- C. Treasure Island
- D. Jungle Book

Question 22

Is the statement below True or False?

In Scotland Angloromani is spoken in some parts of the Highlands and Islands.

Question 23

What were round barrows?

- A. Defences during the Second World War
- B. Bronze Age tombs where they buried their dead
- C. An innovation of the industrial revolution
- D. A popular music group of the 1960s

Question 24

Which of these statements is correct?

- A. In 1215 King John was forced by his noblemen to agree to a charter of rights called Magna Carta.
- B. In 1215 King Charles I was forced by his noblemen to agree to a charter of rights called Magna Carta.

Practice Test 20 – Answers

Question 1 - True

Question 2 - True

Question 3 - B & C

Question 4 - True

Question 5 - A

Question 6 - A

Question 7 - A

Question 8 - A

Question 9 - True

Question 10 - B

Question 11 - B & C

Question 12 - A

Question 13 - A & D

Question 14 - D

Question 15 - D

Question 16 - B

Question 17 - A

Question 18 - B

Question 19 - A & B

Question 20 - B & C

Question 21 - B & D

Question 22 - False

Question 23 - B

Question 24 - A

PRACTICE TEST 21

Question 1

Is the statement below True or False?

During the Elizabethan Age the British Empire became the largest empire the world has ever seen.

Question 2

At which battle in Ireland in 1690 was James II decisively defeated by William III?

    A. The Battle of Sedgemoor

    B. The Battle of the Boyne

    C. The Battle of Newton Butler

    D. The Battle of Cavan

Question 3

Who decides on the penalty if the jury finds the defendant guilty?

    A. The jury

    B. The judge

    C. The prosecuting lawyer

    D. The Home Secretary

Question 4

Is the statement below True or False?

The Man Booker Prize for fiction is awarded annually for the best fiction novel written by an author from the Commonwealth.

Question 5

As an untrained volunteer in what TWO ways can you help hospitals?

    A. You can register as a driver

    B. You can register as a paramedic

    C. You can register as a blood donor

    D. You can register as an organ donor

Question 6

Which of these statements is correct?

    A. New social classes appeared after the Black Death including owners of large areas of land, gentry.

    B. New social classes appeared during the Enlightenment including owners of large areas of land, gentry.

Question 7

Is the statement below True or False?

The War of the Roses ended at the Battle of Bosworth Field in 1485.

Question 8

Why was Hadrian's Wall built?

    A. To keep out the Normans

    B. To keep out the Romans

    C. To keep out the Vikings

    D. To keep out the Picts

Question 9

Which of these statements is correct?

    A. More women than men study at university.

    B. More men than women study at university.

Question 10

Which TWO people have held the title of 'Lord Protector'?

    A. James Stuart

    B. Charles Stuart

    C. Oliver Cromwell

    D. Richard Cromwell

Question 11

Which of these statements is correct?

    A. St Andrews in Scotland is known as the home of golf

    B. Grantham in England is known as the home of golf

Question12

How is Charles II supposed to have escaped following the battle of Worcester?

    A. By hiding in an Oak tree

    B. By dressing as a woman

    C. By hiding in a well

    D. By bribing his captors

Question 13

Is the statement below True or False?

By law, radio and television coverage of the political parties must be balanced.

Question14

Which of these statements is correct?

    A. You must be at least 17 years old to drive a car or motorcycle and you must have a driving licence to drive on public roads.

    B. You must be at least 18 years old to drive a car or motorcycle and you must have a driving licence to drive on public roads.

Question 15

Which of these statements is correct?

    A. If you are self-employed you need to pay tax through a system called 'Self-Assessment'.

    B. If you are self-employed you need to pay tax through a system called Pay as You Earn (PAYE).

Question 16

Which of these statements is correct?

    A. Sutton Hoo in Suffolk is the burial place of an Anglo-Saxon king.

    B. Sutton Hoo in Norfolk is the burial place of an Iron Age king.

Question 17

Is the statement below True or False?

The UK has hosted the Olympic Games just once (2012).

Question18

What was the large fleet of ships sent to conquer England and restore Catholism, defeated by the English in 1588 under the reign of Elizabeth I?

    A. The Spanish Armada

    B. The Spanish Flotilla

    C. The Spanish Grand Fleet

    D. The Spanish Convoy

Question 19

Where is the Cowes sailing event?

    A. Guernsey

    B. The Isle of Man

    C. The Isle of Wight

    D. Skye

Question 20

Whose works include The Planets?

    A. Gustav Holst (1874-1934)

    B. Benjamin Britten (1913-76)

    C. Henry Purcell (1659-95)

    D. Sir William Walton (1902-83)

Question 21

What did the Human Rights Act of 1998 incorporate into UK law?

   A. The International Convention on the Elimination of All Forms of Racial Discrimination

   B. The European Convention on Human Rights

   C. The European Convention on Extradition

   D. The European Convention on the Rights of Refugees and Migrants

Question 22

Who is often regarded as the founder of modern nursing?

   A. Jessica Ennis

   B. Florence Nightingale

   C. Emmeline Pankhurst

   D. Margaret Thatcher

Question 23

Which was the first war to be extensively covered in the news media through news stories and photographs?

   A. The Zulu War

   B. The Boer War

   C. The First World War

   D. The Crimean War

Question 24

On which day do lovers traditionally exchange cards and gifts?

   A. Valentine's day

   B. Christmas day

   C. St Swithun's day

   D. Significant other day

Practice Test 21 – Answers

Question 1 - False

Question 2 - B

Question 3 - B

Question 4 - True

Question 5 - C & D

Question 6 - A

Question 7 - True

Question 8 - D

Question 9 - A

Question 10 - C & D

Question 11 - A

Question 12 - A

Question 13 - True

Question 14 - A

Question 15 - A

Question 16 - A

Question 17 - False

Question 18 - A

Question 19 - C

Question 20 - A

Question 21 - B

Question 22 - B

Question 23 - D

Question 24 - A

PRACTICE TEST 22

Question 1

Is the statement below True or False?

The 'Battle of Britain' in July 1916 resulted in about 60,000 casualties on the first day.

Question 2

What is the name of the agreement leading to peace in Northern Ireland, signed in 1998?

    A. The Good Friday Agreement

    B. The Dayton Agreement

    C. The London and Zurich Agreement

    D. The Armistice Agreement

Question 3

Is the statement below True or False?

The Fringe or Edinburg Festival is a showcase of theatre and comedy held annually.

Question 4

Which area is not currently protected against discrimination in the UK?

    A. Age

    B. Disability

    C. Race

    D. Social class

Question 5

Is the statement below True or False?

Civil law is used to settle disputes between individuals or groups.

Question 6

Which of these statements is correct?

    A. The UK is divided into Parliamentary constituencies.

    B. The UK is divided into Royal constituencies.

Question 7

What are TWO of the British values and responsibilities?

    A. To support the armed forces

    B. To obey and respect the law

    C. To respect and preserve the environment

    D. To pay your taxes on time

Question 8

Which of these statements is correct?

    A. Britain and France developed Concorde, the world's only supersonic passenger aircraft.

    B. Britain and America developed Concorde, the world's only supersonic passenger aircraft.

Question 9

Which TWO castles from the Middle Ages are still in use?

    A. Windsor

    B. Vindolanda

    C. Shrewsbury

    D. Edinburgh

Question 10

Which of these statements is correct?

    A. The Lord of the Rings by JRR Tolkien was voted the country's best loved novel in 2003.

    B. The Hobbit by JRR Tolkien was voted the country's best loved novel in 2003.

Question 11

Which are the TWO famous British places of interest?

A. Leaning Tower of Pisa

B. The Giant's Causeway

C. Trevi Fountain

D. London Eye

Question 12

Which of these statements is correct?

A. The official homes of the Prime Minister are 10 Downing Street and Chequers.

B. The official homes of the Chancellor of the Exchequer are 10 Downing Street and Chequers.

Question 13

Which Scottish Clan were all killed at Glencoe because they were late in taking an oath to the king?

A. The Campbell's

B. The MacDonald's

C. The MacDougall's

D. The MacLeod's

Question 14

Is the statement below True or False?

Father's day is the third Saturday in July.

Question 15

What were 'pocket boroughs'?

A. Constituencies that are entirely controlled by the crown

B. Constituencies controlled by a single wealthy family

C. Constituencies with a tiny electorate

D. Constituencies on an island

Question 16

What nationality were the parents of author Roald Dahl (1916-90)

    A. Swedish

    B. Austrian

    C. Norwegian

    D. Syrian

Question 17

How many days a week do most shops open?

    A. Four days a week

    B. Five days a week

    C. Six days a week

    D. Seven days a week

Question 18

Which of these statements is correct?

    A. Bradley Wiggins is a cyclist who became the first ever Briton to win the Tour de France in 2012.

    B. Chris Hoy is a cyclist who became the first ever Briton to win the Tour de France in 2012.

Question 19

What was an important part for movies such as *In Which We Serve* during the Second World War?

    A. To inform the public

    B. To boost morale

    C. To encourage people to volunteer

    D. To spread false information

Question 20

Is the statement below True or False?

Sir Francis Drake was one of the first to sail right around the world in his ship the *Golden Hind.*

Question 21

What is female genital mutilation also known as?

    A. Cutting or female circumcision

    B. Myomectomy

    C. Dilatation and curettage

    D. Hysterectomy

Question 22

What TWO things do we know about the Easter Rising of 1916?

    A. Irish nationalists rose against the British in Dublin

    B. The leaders were executed under military law

    C. Scottish nationalists rose against the British in the Highlands

    D. The leaders were transported to Australia

Question 23

Which of these statements is correct?

    A. A quarter of the population of England died during the Black death.

    B. A third of the population of England died during the Black death.

Question 24

What is William Wilberforce famous for?

    A. He played an important part in changing the law and in turning public opinion against the slave trade

    B. He was a famous cricketer

    C. He directed a number of famous British films

    D. He was a well-known landscape painter most famous for his works of Dedham Vale

Practice Test 22 – Answers

Question 1 - False

Question 2 - A

Question 3 - True

Question 4 - D

Question 5 - True

Question 6 - A

Question 7 - B & C

Question 8 - A

Question 9 - A & D

Question 10 - A

Question 11 - B & D

Question 12 - A

Question 13 - B

Question 14 - False

Question 15 - B

Question 16 - C

Question 17 - D

Question 18 - A

Question 19 - B

Question 20 - True

Question 21 - A

Question 22 - A & B

Question 23 - B

Question 24 - A

PRACTICE TEST 23

Question 1

Britain played a leading role in a coalition of forces involved in liberating which Middle Eastern country in 1990?

    A. Kuwait

    B. Qatar

    C. Saudi Arabia

    D. Yemen

Question 2

What TWO things did Sake Dean Mahomet introduce to the UK?

    A. The curry house

    B. Shampooing

    C. Fish and chips

    D. The knife and fork

Question 3

Is the statement below True or False?

Roast beef, served with potatoes and vegetables is associated with England

Question 4

Where must you display an R plate for one year after passing the driving test?

    A. England

    B. Scotland

    C. Wales

    D. Northern Ireland

Question 5

Is the statement below True or False?

Prime Minister's Questions takes place every week while Parliament is sitting.

Question 6

Which of these statements is correct?

- A. Winston Churchill was Britain's Prime Minister and War Leader during the Second World War.
- B. Harold Wilson was Britain's Prime Minister and War Leader during the Second World War.

Question 7

Which Olympic gold did Jessica Ennis win at the London Olympics in 2012?

- A. The 100 meters
- B. The javelin
- C. The heptathlon
- D. The long jump

Question 8

Is the statement below True or False?

Sir Robert Walpole was the first Prime Minister.

Question 9

Which of these statements is correct?

- A. Lake Windermere is the largest expanse of fresh water in mainland Britain.
- B. Loch Lomond is the largest expanse of fresh water in mainland Britain.

Question 10

Which TWO political parties formed a coalition government in 2010?

- A. Liberal
- B. Labour
- C. Conservative
- D. Green

Question 11

Which of these statements is correct?

    A. The London Eye was built as part of the UK's celebrations of the new millennium.

    B. The Angel of the North was built as part of the UK's celebrations of the new millennium.

Question 12

When are all young people in the UK sent a National Insurance number?

    A. Soon after a birth is registered

    B. Just before their 10th birthday

    C. Just before their 16th birthday

    D. Just before their 18th birthday

Question 13

Is the statement below True or False?

After 1833, 2 million Indian and Chinese workers were employed to replace freed slaves.

Question 14

Which TWO ingredients are found in Haggis?

    A. Offal

    B. A sheep's stomach

    C. Fish

    D. Chicken wings

Question 15

Which Prime Minister is famous for his 'wind of change' speech about decolonization and independence of the countries of the Empire?

    A. Harold Macmillan

    B. Neville Chamberlain

    C. Harold Wilson

    D. John Major

Question 16

Name TWO of the Allied powers of World War I

    A. Germany

    B. Austro-Hungary

    C. France

    D. Japan

Question 17

Which is the oldest continuously working film studio in the world?

    A. Pinewood Studios

    B. Ealing Studios

    C. Cricklewood Studios

    D. Lime Grove Studios

Question 18

What building is the dominant feature of the skyline in Edinburgh?

    A. The Scott Memorial

    B. Arthur's Seat

    C. Holyrood

    D. Edinburgh castle

Question 19

When must you take your car for a Ministry of Transport (MOT) test?

    A. Every year if your car is more than 3 years old

    B. Every 3 years if your car is more than 3 years old

    C. Every 5 years

    D. Every 6 years

Question 20

What is the taxation system called for those who are self-employed?

A. Self-assessment

B. PAYE (Pay as You Earn)

C. MTDD (Monthly Tax Direct Debit)

D. Tax credits

Question 21

Is the statement below True or False?

In the 18th century political cartoons attacking politicians, the monarchy and Royal Family became popular.

Question 22

What TWO things do we know about civil servants?

A. They are selected from the armed forces

B. They are chosen on merit

C. They are politically neutral

D. They are political appointees

Question 23

Which of these statements is correct?

A. British scientists such as Ernest Rutherford took part in the Manhattan Project which developed the Atom Bomb.

B. British scientists such as Keith Campbell took part in the Oppenheim Project which developed the Atom Bomb.

Question 24

In the middle of the 19th century which crop failed in Ireland leading to a famine where a million people died of disease and starvation?

A. The wheat crop

B. The potato crop

C. The barley crop

D. The maize crop

Practice Test 23 – Answers

Question 1 - A

Question 2 - A & B

Question 3 - True

Question 4 - D

Question 5 - True

Question 6 - A

Question 7 - C

Question 8 - True

Question 9 - B

Question 10 - A & C

Question 11 - A

Question 12 - C

Question 13 - True

Question 14 - A & B

Question 15 - A

Question 16 - C & D

Question 17 - B

Question 18 - D

Question 19 - A

Question 20 - A

Question 21 - True

Question 22 - B & D

Question 23 - A

Question 24 - B

PRACTICE TEST 24

Question 1

Is the statement below True or False?

The annual British Academy Film Awards hosted by BAFTA are the British equivalent of the Oscars.

Question 2

What TWO things does the Carding process produce?

    A. Yarn

    B. Steel

    C. Petrol

    D. Fabric

Question 3

Is the statement below True or False?

If the monarch dies or abdicates there is an election.

Question 4

Under William and Mary how often did a new Parliament have to be elected?

    A. Whenever the king needed to raise money

    B. At least every ten years

    C. At least every three years

    D. On the death of the reigning monarch

Question 5

Which of these statements is correct?

    A. St Augustine led missionaries from Rome and became the first Archbishop of Canterbury.

    B. St Paul led missionaries from Rome and became the first Archbishop of Canterbury.

Question 6

Which of these statements is correct?

    A. The Domesday Book, commissioned by William the Conqueror, contains a list of all the towns and villages in England and lists who lived where, who owned the land and what animals they owned.

    B. The Domesday Register, commissioned by Henry VIII, contains a list of all the towns and villages in England and lists who lived where, who owned the land and what animals they owned.

Question 7

Is the statement below True or False?

On 28 June 1914, Archduke Franz Ferdinand of Austria was assassinated setting off a chain of events leading to the First World War (1914-1918).

Question 8

When is an arranged marriage acceptable in the UK?

    A. When both parties agree to the marriage

    B. When both parents agree to the marriage

    C. When the Home Office agrees to the marriage

    D. When a lawyer attends the marriage

Question 9

Which of these statements is correct?

    A. Morecambe and Wise were music hall comedians who went on to become stars of television.

    B. Watson and Crick were music hall comedians who went on to become stars of television.

Question 10

In Ireland which TWO kings extended English control outside 'the pale'?

    A. Henry VII

    B. Henry VIII

    C. Richard I

    D. George III

Question 11

Which of these statements is correct?

    A. The National Anthem of the UK is 'God Save the Queen'.

    B. The National Anthem of the UK is 'Land of Hope and Glory'.

Question 12

Between 1680 and 1720 which country did the protestant Huguenot refugees, who had been persecuted for their religion, come from?

    A. Syria

    B. France

    C. Serbia

    D. Vietnam

Question 13

Which period after the Norman Conquest up until 1485 was a time of almost constant war?

    A. The Tudors

    B. The Stuarts

    C. The Reformation

    D. The Middle Ages

Question 14

What are TWO types of criminal court?

    A. Crown court

    B. County court

    C. Sheriff court

    D. Constituency court

Question 15

Which TWO did Oliver Cromwell achieve?

    A. He established the authority of the English Parliament in Ireland

    B. He defeated Charles II at the battles of Bannockburn and Flodden

    C. He became King

    D. He became Lord Protector

Question 16

Who wrote Oliver Twist and Great Expectations?

    A. Evelyn Waugh

    B. Charles Dickens

    C. Thomas Hardy

    D. Kingsley Amis

Question 17

Is the statement below True or False?

Prime Minister Clement Attlee introduced the Welfare State.

Question 18

Which of these statements is correct?

    A. You have to be 16 or more to participate in the National Lottery.

    B. You have to be 18 or more to participate in the National Lottery.

Question 19

Which of these is not a civil matter?

    A. Personal injury

    B. Breach of contract

    C. Divorce

    D. Theft

Question 20

Which TWO regional languages are also common in broadcasts in the UK?

    A. Gaelic

    B. Polish

    C. Welsh

    D. French

Question 21

Is the statement below True or False?

David Hockney was an important contributor to the development of IVF (in-vitro fertilization) in the 1960s.

Question 22

Which of these statements is correct?

    A. The British Constitution is not written down in any single document and is described as 'unwritten'.

    B. Britain has a written constitution.

Question 23

What is the name given to the land formation of columns made from volcanic lava on the north-east coast of Northern Ireland?

    A. The Giant's Causeway

    B. The Devil's Punch Bowl

    C. Durdle Door

    D. Cerne Abbas

Question 24

What is John Maynard Keynes known for?

    A. New theories of economics

    B. As inventor of the hover craft

    C. As a painter of landscapes

    D. His work on the jet engine

Practice Test 24 – Answers

Question 1 - True

Question 2 - A & D

Question 3 - False

Question 4 - C

Question 5 - A

Question 6 - A

Question 7 - True

Question 8 - A

Question 9 - A

Question 10 - A & B

Question 11 - A

Question 12 - B

Question 13 - D

Question 14 - A & C

Question 15 - A & D

Question 16 - B

Question 17 - True

Question 18 - A

Question 19 - D

Question 20 - A & C

Question 21 - False

Question 22 - A

Question 23 - A

Question 24 - A

PRACTICE TEST 25

Question 1
Is the statement below True or False?

Sir Christopher Wren developed the Tower of London.

Question 2
What are the TWO systems that HMRC use to collect tax?
- A. Pay as You Earn (PAYE)
- B. Self-Assessment
- C. Direct Assessment
- D. Means Based Earnings Deduction (MBTE)

Question 3
Is the statement below True or False?

The official homes of the Prime Minister are 10 Downing Street and Chequers.

Question 4
Who wrote the James Bond books?
- A. Ernst Stavro Blofeld
- B. Peter Wright
- C. Ian Fleming
- D. John le Carré

Question 5
Which of these statements is correct?
- A. King Harold died at the Battle of Hastings.
- B. King Harold died at the Battle of Marston Moor.

Question 6

Which of these statements is correct?

    A. St George is the patron saint of England and St George's day is 23 April.

    B. St Patrick is the patron saint of England and St Patrick's day is 23 April.

Question 7

Which of these statements is correct?

    A. In Scotland a jury has 15 members.

    B. In Scotland a jury has 12 members.

Question 8

Where did the Vikings come from?

    A. Ireland

    B. France

    C. Sweden and the Netherlands

    D. Denmark and Norway

Question 9

Which of these statements is correct?

    A. In England, Wales and Northern Ireland most minor criminal offences are dealt with in a Magistrates Court.

    B. In England, Wales and Northern Ireland most minor criminal offences are dealt with in a Sheriffs Court.

Question 10

How old do you have to be before you can legally purchase alcohol?

    A. 14 years old

    B. 16 years old

    C. 18 years old

    D. 21 years old

Question 11

Is the statement below True or False?

On Victory in Europe day there is a two minute silence at 11.00am and wreaths are laid at the Cenotaph in London, Whitehall.

Question 12

Which country did the English kings fight a very long war with, called the Hundred Years War?

    A. Spain

    B. The Netherlands

    C. Germany

    D. France

Question 13

Is the statement below True or False?

Leading fashion designers include Jessica Ennis, Jane Austen and Evelyn Waugh.

Question 14

Is the statement below True or False?

In May 2010 no political party won an overall majority in the General Election and the Conservative and Liberal Democrat parties formed a coalition.

Question 15

What TWO things must you be over 18 before you can do?

    A. Drive a car

    B. Buy alcohol

    C. Purchase a National Lottery ticket

    D. Go into betting shops or gambling clubs

Question 16

What system of land ownership did the Normans use?

    A. Feudalism

    B. Native title

    C. Life estate

    D. Allodial

Question 17

What TWO things do we know about Admiral Lord Nelson?

    A. He was killed at the Battle of Trafalgar

    B. He married Lady Hornblower

    C. His ship was HMS Victory

    D. He came from a rich aristocratic family

Question 18

Which West-End show has the longest initial run of any show in history?

    A. The Mousetrap

    B. Les Miserable

    C. Cats

    D. The Mikado

Question 19

If you are arrested what must a police officer tell you?

    A. The reason for the arrest and that you will be able to seek legal advice

    B. The reason for the arrest

    C. The reason for the arrest and their police number

    D. The reason for the arrest, that you will be able to seek legal advice, and their police number

Question 20

Which of these statements is correct?

    A. The population in the UK in 2010 was just over 30 million.

    B. The population in the UK in 2010 was just over 62 million.

Question 21

Which TWO cities in Japan did America drop the atomic bomb on?

    A. Hiroshima

    B. Nagasaki

    C. Kyoto

    D. Tokyo

Question 22

Which of these statements is correct?

    A. The War of the Roses was fought between supporters of two families 'The House of York' and the 'House of Lancaster'

    B. The War of the Roses was fought between supporters of two families 'The House of Tudor' and the 'House of Stuart'.

Question 23

What were the TWO most important planes used by the Royal Air Force in the Battle of Britain

    A. The Spitfire

    B. The Hurricane

    C. The Lancaster

    D. The Sopwith Camel

Question 24

Which Prime Minister was voted the greatest Briton of all time by the public in 2002?

    A. Clement Attlee

    B. Winston Churchill

    C. Tony Blair

    D. Harold Wilson

Practice Test 25 – Answers

Question 1 - False

Question 2 - A & B

Question 3 - True

Question 4 - C

Question 5 - A

Question 6 - A

Question 7 - A

Question 8 - D

Question 9 - A

Question 10 - C

Question 11 - False

Question 12 - D

Question 13 - False

Question 14 - True

Question 15 - B & D

Question 16 - A

Question 17 - A & C

Question 18 - A

Question 19 - A

Question 20 - B

Question 21 - A & B

Question 22 - A

Question 23 - A & B

Question 24 - B

Also available from Garuda Publications

The Life in the UK Test Handbook:

Essential independent study guide on the test for 'Settlement in the UK' and 'British Citizenship', 4th edition

'Contains everything you'll need to pass the test'

- The official study material for the test from '*Life in the United Kingdom: A guide for new residents, 3rd edition*'
- 'Statements that are True' to help you revise
- A full practice test
- Glossary of essential words and phrases
- Listing of all people mentioned in the study material
- Checklist of the conflicts mentioned in the study material
- Table of all the battles mentioned in the study material
- A list of key documents and legislation in the guidance
- Diary checklist showing the annual calendar events; and
- An historic UK timeline shows key events that you may be tested on
- Colour illustrations and diagrams throughout

The Life in the UK Test Handbook: in Thai and English, 4th edition

Essential independent study guide in Thai and English on the test for 'Settlement in the UK' and 'British Citizenship'.

*   This fourth edition contains a full Thai translation of the official study material for the Life in the UK Test '*Life in the United Kingdom: A Guide for New Residents, 3rd edition*' together with the original English text.
*   Revision material is also provided in Thai and English including 'statements that are true' and a practice test.
*   As well as material about the test itself the book includes information on the visa categories and process that lead to settlement in the UK and British Citizenship.
*   For those that go on to pass the test there is also information on the types of questions asked at an interview for a British Passport

The Life in the UK Test Handbook: in Vietnamese and English

In Vietnamese and English
Bảng tiếng Việt và tiếng Anh

the
Life in the UK
Test Handbook

Sổ Tay Kì Thi 'Life in the UK'

The essential guide
on the tests for 'Settlement in the UK'
and 'British Citizenship'

Includes the official study materials
and their Vietnamese translation

Essential independent study guide in Vietnamese and English on the test for 'Settlement in the UK' and 'British Citizenship'.

- This second edition contains a full Vietnamese translation of the official study material for the Life in the UK Test '*Life in the United Kingdom: A Guide for New Residents, 3rd edition*' together with the original English text.
- Revision material is also provided in Vietnamese and English including 'statements that are true' and a practice test.
- As well as material about the test itself the book includes information on the visa categories and process that lead to settlement in the UK and British Citizenship.
- For those that go on to pass the test there is also information on the types of questions asked at an interview for a British Passport

The Life in the UK Test E-learning course

The complete online training resource for the Life in the UK Test is found at:
Training.GarudaPublications.com

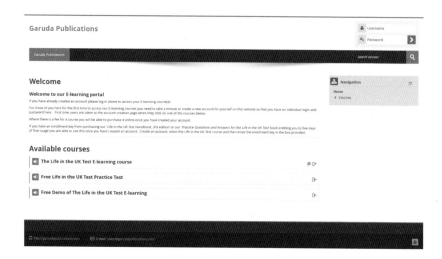

- Interactive content
- Modular structure – study the sections in any order
- Simple course navigation
- 24/7 access
- Progress tracking
- Includes the official study material – from *'Life in the United Kingdom: a guide for new residents (3rd edition)'*
- Hundreds of practice questions
- Guaranteed pass scheme (If you don't pass first time study free until you do)
- Optimized for PCs, tablets and mobile devices

Purchasers of this Questions and Answers guide are currently entitled to free access to the E-learning course and practice and answers. Simply create an account at **Training.Garudapublications.com.** Then use the enrollment key **Garuda2017** to gain free access to the E-learning training and practice tests - currently for up to 5 days. *Garuda Publications reserves the right to vary the free term and enrollment keys without prior notice.*